Y0-CCH-423

$2.60

BY THE SAME AUTHOR

INTERNATIONAL GOLD
MOVEMENTS
Second Edition
Pp. xiv + 168.   1931
7*s*. 6*d*. net.

THE BANK FOR INTERNATIONAL
SETTLEMENTS
Third Edition
Pp. xv + 267.   1932
Price 10*s*. 6*d*. net.

THE FIGHT FOR FINANCIAL
SUPREMACY
Third Edition
Pp. xvi + 180.   1931
Price 7*s*. 6*d*. net.

BEHIND THE SCENES OF
INTERNATIONAL FINANCE
Third Impression
Pp. xviii + 154.   1932
Price 7*s*. 6*d*. net.

FINANCE AND POLITICS
Pp. x + 139.   1932
Price 7*s*. 6*d*. net.

THE WORLD
ECONOMIC CRISIS

MACMILLAN AND CO., Limited
LONDON · BOMBAY · CALCUTTA · MADRAS
MELBOURNE

THE MACMILLAN COMPANY
NEW YORK · BOSTON · CHICAGO
DALLAS · ATLANTA · SAN FRANCISCO

THE MACMILLAN COMPANY
OF CANADA LIMITED
TORONTO

WILSON SCHMIDT LIBRARY
PUBLIC CHOICE CENTER

THE WORLD ECONOMIC CRISIS

1929-1932

BY

PAUL EINZIG

MACMILLAN AND CO., LIMITED
ST. MARTIN'S STREET, LONDON

1932

COPYRIGHT

First Edition, 1931
Second Edition, February 1932
Third Edition, September 1932

PRINTED IN GREAT BRITAIN
BY R. & R. CLARK, LIMITED, EDINBURGH

338
Einzig

PREFACE TO THIRD EDITION

DURING the six months that have elapsed since the revision of this book for second edition there has been no fundamental change in the international economic situation. After the turn of the year the crisis became somewhat less violent, though from time to time there was a new crash in some part of the world to aggravate the situation. Moreover, the fall of world prices continued unabated, and so has the decline of world trade caused by various restrictions and by the contraction of the purchasing power of consumers. At the same time, the psychological factor seems to have changed for the better to some extent. Apparently mankind is becoming increasingly accustomed to the crisis, and its nerves are now able to withstand shocks which a year ago would inevitably have caused a panic. Thus the comparative ease with which the world got over the collapse of the Kreuger and Toll group speaks well for its resisting capacity.

The political factor continues to be the main source of uncertainty. It is generally felt that from a purely economic point of view there is no reason why a recovery should not take place as soon as the adverse political factor is eliminated. The fall of commodity and security prices has obviously been beyond the limit up to which it can be justified by economic considerations; there is thus a fair scope for recovery. The weak and unsound elements have been eliminated from economic life, and to some extent the surplus stocks have been liquidated. If only the world can settle down to peaceful co-operation, prosperity is bound to return.

In accordance with the changes which have taken place since December last, this new edition has been revised and brought up to date. As it covers the first half of 1932, the title of the book has been modified accordingly.

P. E.

20 BISHOPSGATE, E.C.2
June, 1932

PREFACE TO SECOND EDITION

SINCE the first edition of this book was written the international economic situation has undergone a fundamental change for the worse. In May 1931 there was reason to hope that the crisis would take its course without culminating in a disaster, and that in the course of time a process of readjustment would restore the situation that existed previous to the boom. The events of the last eight months, however, have frustrated these hopes. The economic crisis has developed into a financial crisis of unprecedented gravity which has shaken the very foundations of our economic system. Although there is no reason to cease to hope for the return of prosperity, it will be long before the wounds caused by the crisis are completely healed. In the spring it was reasonable to assume that a normal process of readjustment would bring about the desired recovery, but at present it appears that normal conditions cannot be expected to return without a fundamental reorganisation of the economic system.

The changes in the situation since the first edition was written has made it necessary to make considerable changes in the book. Parts I. and II., which describe the crisis and analyse its causes, have needed little modification : the author's task here has been confined to bringing the material up to date. On the other hand, Part III., which indicates the way to recovery, has been almost completely rewritten. At the present stage, when the outlook is as obscure as ever, it is not an enviable task to attempt to indicate the way out. The situation changes from day to day, and any suggestion made at this stage may become hopelessly out of date by the time the new edition has appeared. For this reason many of the author's conclusions in this part are necessarily vague and subjected to many reserves.

New chapters have been added on "Overcapitalisation"; on "The Financial Crisis" as distinct from the economic crisis; on the chances and methods of a "Restoration of Confidence"; on the inevitability of a "National Solution" if attempts at a solution on international lines break down; and on "Inflation or Deflation" as the way out. The Appendices, describing the crisis in individual countries, have been brought up to date.

The last part of the book, dealing with the question as to how to avoid the recurrence of the crisis, has been left entirely unchanged. The author is convinced, more than ever, that the only hope for mankind to save civilisation in its present form is closer co-operation in every sphere of economic life.

P. E.

20 Bishopsgate, E.C.2
    December, 1931

PREFACE TO FIRST EDITION

IT has become a habit to regard the present economic crisis as something highly mysterious, the explanation of which—if indeed an explanation can be given—is too abstruse to be intelligible to the average man. In reality, however, there is nothing mysterious about the crisis. The aim of this book is to dispel the atmosphere of mystery which surrounds the causes of the crisis, and to make the readers understand that, complex as it is, the explanation can certainly be understood by anybody of average intelligence. It is, indeed, most desirable that those who are affected by the crisis—and this means practically everybody—should be in a position to understand its causes and appreciate its consequences. If the crisis were understood more widely, this would do much to hasten recovery, and would avert the danger of complete economic chaos; so long as the crisis is regarded by the majority of the public as something supernatural —or, at any rate, something as entirely beyond human control as an earthquake or a cyclone—they may be inclined to exaggerate its dangers. If, however, they are in a position to explain the crisis to themselves, they are less likely to lose their sense of proportion, and will find it easier to wait patiently for the advent of better days.

The author attempts to explain, in non-technical language, the causes of the economic crisis; he attempts to assess the chances of recovery; and he suggests ways by which recovery could be hastened and by which the recurrence of the crisis could be avoided in future. The book is addressed to the man in the street; it does not claim to be a scientific treatise. At the risk of displeasing academic critics, the author has refrained from including in his book charts, statistical tables, and a mass of quotations from works by eminent authors, which may look impressive, but certainly do not make the book more readable. The author has no ambition to establish a new theory of crises, nor to support any particular existing theory to the exclusion of the others. He is not trying to find a scapegoat for the troubles, nor to exonerate from blame any particular group or section which has been attacked. Although he is critical towards various interests which may have contributed to some extent towards the crisis, his book is not intended to be an indictment. Its main conclusion is that the crisis was largely due to inadequate co-operation between various economic interests. It is due largely to this want of collaboration that, at the time of writing, the crisis is still in full swing with no immediate prospects of recovery.

The author lays stress upon the necessity for co-operation, both within the borders of any one country and between various countries, in order to bring the crisis to an end and in order to avoid similar troubles in the future. Those who expect any spectacular suggestions of miraculous remedies may find the book disappointing. The suggestions that are made constitute obvious common-sense solutions, which are, none the less, too frequently overlooked.

It is high time that the public took greater interest in the discussion of the causes, effects, and remedies of the crisis. Their discussion should cease to be the sacred privilege of the high priests of economic science; it should be open to everybody who is affected by the crisis. If this book provides some help to the uninitiated in this respect, the author feels he has attained his end.

P. E.

20 BISHOPSGATE, E.C.2
May, 1931

CONTENTS

PART I

INTRODUCTORY

CHAPTER I

CHAPTER II

PART II

CAUSES OF THE CRISIS

CHAPTER III

CHAPTER IV

PART III
THE WAY OUT

PART IV
FUTURE PROSPECTS

APPENDICES

PART I

INTRODUCTORY

CHAPTER I

FOREWORD

DURING the period between 1922 and 1929 the world made remarkable progress on the way to recovery from the chaotic situation created by the war. Conditions were gradually approaching the state which we had been accustomed before the war to regard as normal. Governments succeeded in balancing their budgets, and many of them began to reduce their debts. Inflation for the purpose of financing budgetary deficits had ceased all over the world. Most currencies were stabilised; in 1929 the number of countries with a stable currency was greater than before the war. The abnormal restrictions upon imports, exports, and domestic trade, imposed during the war, had been removed in practically every country. The price level became almost as stable as in pre-war days, which did not, of course, mean absolute stability, for, throughout history, prices have been moving either upwards or downwards. Between 1922 and 1929 there was a slowly declining tendency in gold prices, but it was not sufficiently pronounced to interfere with economic progress. Although the world prices in 1929 were about 40 per cent above the pre-war level, many economists were inclined to regard this as a normal state of affairs in accordance with permanent changes which have taken place since 1914, and which, in their opinion, would have taken place even if there had been no world war.

It is true that this normal economic situation was not quite restored even eleven years after the cessation of hostilities. The increase of tariffs in many countries prevented international trade from returning to its accustomed channels. Discrepancies between the price levels of various countries, due largely to conditions in which their respective currencies were stabilised, were not altogether readjusted. The fixing of new frontiers in Europe, changes in production and consumption, and various other circumstances, brought about dislocations from the pre-war state of affairs. There was the disturbing factor of maldistribution of gold; of abnormal differences between interest rates in various countries; and, above all, of the abnormal state of international indebtedness brought about by the war. It was generally realised that, unless and until these maladjustments had been solved, normal conditions could not be said to have been restored. There was obviously some progress towards the desired end: the temporary dislocations in trade were gradually being eliminated, while the dislocations of a permanent nature forced a process of adjustment, as a result of which there was reason to hope for an establishment of a new state of equilibrium. Much progress had been made towards the adjustment of reparation claims to a figure at which they ceased to constitute a source of danger to equilibrium. The flow of capital from the rich to the poor countries tended gradually to eliminate the discrepancies in interest rates caused by the destruction of wealth through war and inflation. Endeavours to develop international co-operation in order to solve the problems of gold and interest rates were making headway.

In such circumstances it was only natural that the

world should develop some optimism as to the economic outlook. It was taken for granted that the progress made during the seven years 1923–1929 would continue, and that nothing but another world war—a most unlikely contingency—or a disaster of similar magnitude, could check the process of recovery. It was confidently anticipated that, in the course of another few years, conditions would once more become normal in the pre-war sense of the term. A convalescent world was inclined to overlook the fact that, apart from the seriousness of the illness from which it was recovering, there existed other sources of trouble which might cause a relapse in its recovery. Few people remembered that even before the war everything was not ideal, as economic life was disturbed from time to time by violent crises, and that, much as conditions had changed since then, we had no right to assume that they had changed sufficiently to eliminate the factors which then gave us trouble. The occasional timid warnings of a few economists were not sufficiently convincing to attract much attention.

The economic crisis which began towards the end of 1929, and which developed into a violent financial crisis in 1931, took the world completely by surprise. It descended upon us gradually, and its gravity was not fully realised until the summer of 1931. Until then it was regarded as a depression, due to the Wall Street crash, which would soon pass away. When, in the autumn of 1930, it threatened to culminate in a panic, popular as well as expert opinion realised that we were faced with an economic crisis as grave as any we have experienced in modern times. Confidence, which until then had been well maintained, gave way to strong pessimism. After several critical months the public seems to have calmed down.

Early in 1931 people began to think that the worst was over. There appeared indeed to be many signs of economic recovery; commodity prices began to rise, and Stock Exchanges assumed a more cheerful tone. The runs on banks which caused considerable concern in several countries towards the end of 1930 subsided, and abnormal gold movements appeared to have come to an end. It was widely expected, and not altogether without reason, that within a few months, or a year at the most, we should be able to breathe once more freely.

Unfortunately these anticipations proved to be too optimistic. The announcement of the Austro-German Customs Union scheme resulted in a nervous tension in the international atmosphere, which did not fail to produce its effect upon the economic situation. The difficulties of the Creditanstalt proved to be a starting-point for an international banking crisis of unprecedented severity, which again resulted in a currency crisis culminating in the suspension of the gold standard in Great Britain and a number of other countries. Commodity prices began to fall again after their temporary recovery in 1931, and Stock Exchange quotations declined to new low records. Unemployment increased in practically every country, and the exchange restrictions, together with new tariffs introduced in various countries, have resulted in a complete disorganisation of international trade. The number of bankruptcies in most countries, and the amounts involved, have reached unprecedented figures, and the depreciation of every kind of investment has inflicted heavy losses upon large classes of the population.

At the beginning of 1932 there was a slight improvement in the international situation. The wave of banking crises subsided, and, contrary to anticipations, none of the leading currencies departed from the gold standard. Even the Kreuger crash was unable to bring about a lasting relapse in the sphere of finance. On the other hand, the economic situation had changed from bad to worse. Commodity prices continued to fall; a number of countries have increased their Customs tariffs, and have introduced other kinds of restrictions on trade; exchange restrictions have been further reinforced. As a result, the volume of international trade has fallen in every country.

Although the world crisis has affected in some way millions of people in every country, few of them have any idea at all as to the cause of their troubles. They all feel that something must be fundamentally wrong, but fail to see exactly what it is. It is not as if no explanations had been put forward; on the contrary, it is largely because of the great number of contradictory explanations that the uninitiated are bewildered and are at a loss to know whom to believe. Theoretical economists of great reputation are at pains to make use of the facts of the crisis to justify their own favourite theories. It is indeed amazing to see how the same facts and figures can serve the purpose of proving the most contradictory theories, and how easy it is to produce an intimidating display of statistical tables and charts to prove each one of them. We are told by some authorities that the source of all our troubles is that people have spent too much, but we are told by others that the crisis is due to inadequate spending. Some people blame the Stock Exchanges for all troubles, while others maintain that Stock Exchanges have rendered a useful service by giving an emphatic warning, without which the world would have continued to live in a fool's paradise from which the final awakening would have been even more unpleasant. Agriculture, industries, monetary policy, gold shortage, trade unionism, and all forms of commodity restriction schemes have each in turn been made, by somebody or other, the scapegoat for all troubles. Political parties in every country have made capital out of the crisis to blame the existing Government for having failed to avert the catastrophe, or the previous Government for having failed to make adequate preparations for it. Socialists of the extreme school blame the capitalist system, while Conservatives of the other extreme put all the blame on excessive wages and social legislation. The attacks of demagogues on international finance are, once more, in full swing, while there are many people who regard the Soviet Government as being responsible for everything that is wrong. The orthodox school of pre-war economists are probably the only people who do not blame anybody at all; they look upon the crisis as an inevitable part of the trade cycle which operates, in their opinion, in the same way as it did before the war. Others, again, maintain that the relapse of the price level to its pre-war figure, which caused the crisis, was inevitable. As a contrast to their fatalism, a number of experts and pseudo-experts put forward an amazing variety of suggestions of what ought to have been done to avert the crisis and what should be done to restore prosperity. The great majority of these suggestions are quack remedies which do not deserve serious consideration, and their only effect is to increase the confusion in the mind of the public as to the causes and the nature of the crisis and the way out.

It would serve little useful purpose to prove the one-sidedness of the theories put forward in explanation of the crisis. The problem has to be approached in a constructive and not in a destructive spirit. A great many of the explanations contain some truth. If only those responsible for them would take them for what they are worth, instead of claiming that their theories contain 100 per cent of truth, they would be much more useful in contributing towards finding the right solution. In the subsequent chapters an attempt will be made to provide a survey of the principal explanations of the crisis, so as to enable the reader to form his own opinion as to their respective importance, and to distil from them whatever is worth retaining.

There are two schools of thought as to the nature of the present crisis. According to one school it is merely the recurrence of the cyclical crisis, well known before the war, and its exceptional violence and extension is regarded as merely a difference of degree. According to the other, the present crisis differs fundamentally from any previous crisis. While the cyclical crises during the hundred years or so that preceded the war carried their own corrective tendencies, the present crisis does not seem to set into motion factors bringing about a readjustment. Until the middle of 1931 the first school appeared to be right, because the evolution of the crisis until then showed little if any material difference from past experience. During the second half of 1931, however, the evolution of the crisis indicated the existence of disturbing influences outside the sphere of normal economic tendencies. The political factor has assumed predominant importance, and has become the obvious obstacle to the working of factors which would normally tend to bring about a recovery.

The discovery of the causes of the crisis, interesting as it is, is only a means to an end; its practical aim is to enable us to see whether there is a way out, and whether anything can be done to hasten the process of disentanglement. An enormous variety of suggestions has been made as to how to restore normal conditions. Cranks of all nations—their number is legion—have never been as active as during the last two years. During a period when conditions are more or less normal, they have little chance to find adherents. In times of crisis, however, when the public is at a loss to account for its troubles, and is willing to clutch at every straw, their proposals may not necessarily encounter deaf ears everywhere. The management of economic and financial policies of most countries is, however, in essentially conservative hands, so that no country is likely to become the scene of charlatan experiments. In fact, official quarters usually err on the side of extreme caution, and are reluctant to depart from their routine to hasten recovery. There is, however, a happy medium between adopting the schemes of economic witch-doctors and the fatalistic lethargy that characterises the attitude of both the public and the authorities in every country. As we shall try to show in Part III. of this book, there is much that could be done to hasten the advent of a revival of trade.

At present we are too much absorbed by our existing troubles and problems to have much time for thought as to possible future troubles. It is, however, not untimely to consider the means by which the recurrence of such a crisis could be prevented. Although there may be many devices which could be helpful, we shall try to indicate that the best preventative is co-operation. It will be seen that inadequate co-operation played a prominent part in bringing about, in accentuating, and in prolonging our present crisis. It is through increased co-operation that the end of our troubles could be brought nearer, and it is through increased co-operation that their repetition could be avoided.

CHAPTER II

A BRIEF ACCOUNT OF THE CRISIS

WHEREAS it is usually easy to fix the date of the beginning of a political crisis, it is, as a rule, rather difficult to indicate a date as marking the beginning of an economic crisis. In the case of political crises, there is always some event, a declaration, or an act of some kind, which can be regarded as the starting-point of the trouble. An economic crisis, on the other hand, is the outcome of the operation of slowly working tendencies. The decline of the price level is, in itself, not a crisis; it is only when the rate of decline reaches a certain point that it assumes the characteristics of an economic depression which may eventually become accentuated into a crisis. The increase of unemployment is unquestionably an index of the crisis, but it is very difficult to say at what point it can be said that the stage of depression has developed into a stage of crisis. The growing number of bankruptcies is yet another obvious sign of an economic crisis, but here again the increase of the number of failures and of the amounts involved may be so gradual and fluctuating as to make it impossible to draw the border-line. After all, between, say, 100 and 150 failures during a given period in a given community, the difference may only be one of degree.

It has become a habit to speak of the Wall Street

slump of October 1929 as the starting-point of our
crisis. There is a great deal to be said in favour of this
conception. It is true that the decline of commodity
prices began several months before the Wall Street
slump, and that trade all over the world, and even in
the United States, showed some signs of decline even
before the black days of Wall Street. The Wall Street
crash was, nevertheless, an event of such outstanding
importance that it ought to be regarded as a landmark
in post-war economic history.

At the time of the Wall Street crash few people
realised that we were at the beginning of a prolonged
and severe crisis. It was, in fact, held that the cessation of the unsound speculative boom in Wall Street
would have a beneficial effect on trade all over the
world, as it would release the capital engaged directly
or indirectly in speculation. Even when the fall of
wholesale prices became accentuated during the months
that followed the Wall Street crash, the gravity of the
situation was not immediately realised. It was not until
about a year after that event that the public became
aware that, for the past twelve months, it had been
experiencing a crisis.

Agriculture was the branch of production hardest hit
by the crisis. The effect of the war had been, on the
whole, beneficial to agriculture. Landowners were in
a position in most countries to repay their pre-war
indebtedness in depreciated currency. No farmer has
ever admitted that times were good, but during the few
years ended 1928 they had comparatively little reason
to grumble. Technical improvements—especially the
increased employment of tractors and of the Combine
harvester—tended to reduce the cost of production.
The crisis was indeed precipitated by overproduction,

and came down on agriculture like a bolt from the blue. The record crop in Europe in 1929 was the first factor which was the immediate cause of the trouble. As Europe is the principal consumer of the agricultural products of other continents, the sudden decline of European demand caused serious embarrassment to the agricultural countries outside Europe. Their unsold stocks were accumulating, and the Canadian wheat pool and others, who held back their supplies in the hope of a recovery of prices, eventually had to cut heavy losses. In addition to the general agricultural depression, a crisis existed in several particular groups of agricultural commodities, such as coffee, rubber, and sugar.

The crisis soon began to show itself also in the domain of industrial production. Apart from the United States, France, and one or two smaller countries, industries were none too prosperous, even before the crisis. The effect of the crisis was to reduce the difference between the state of prosperity of the industries of various countries. While conditions became worse in countries such as Great Britain, Italy, and Germany, where industries were depressed even before the Wall Street slump, industrial prosperity in France and the United States gave way to an acute state of depression and heavy unemployment. The industrial depression resulted in a decline in demand for raw materials and fuels, which again reacted upon mining and further accentuated the troubles of agriculture, which was already suffering in consequence of the decline in demand for food, brought about by the increase of unemployment. The decline in the purchasing power of the agricultural population has, in turn, accentuated industrial depression, completing thereby the vicious circle.

Depression in agriculture and industry, falling prices, and the difficulties of selling, resulted in the failure of a large number of commercial and industrial firms. To some extent this was a beneficial process, as it eliminated the mushroom growth of the post-war period, which lost its *raison d'être* once inflation ceased. Unfortunately, however, a large number of well-established firms also failed. In some countries banks adopted a policy of "safety first", and called in their loans regardless of consequences. This was the cause of many failures which otherwise might have been avoided. Wholesale and retail merchants found it increasingly difficult to sell their goods, because, in addition to the reduction of the purchasing power of the public, the latter's willingness to buy within the limits of their purchasing power also declined. Since consumers realised that wholesale prices were falling, they expected a corresponding decline in retail prices, and held off their buying in anticipation of such a decline.

The Stock Exchanges all over the world, which were considerably affected by the Wall Street slump, displayed a persistent declining trend with only temporary rallies. Most of them did not experience as spectacular a slump as that of Wall Street, probably because the boom had not assumed an extent comparable to that of the Wall Street boom. The depreciation of securities all over the world was, nevertheless, enormous, and contributed to the reduction of the purchasing power of the public.

The banks did not escape the effect of the depression. They suffered heavy losses through the failure of many of their customers, and they had to carry the burden of financing frozen stocks of commodities. In countries where banks held shares in industrial and commercial enterprises, they were naturally affected to a particularly great extent as a result of the depreciation of their security holdings. The earning capacity of banks has also declined considerably. There was an all-round falling off of banking activity, and, owing to the persistent fall of interest rates, the margin between borrowing and lending rates also narrowed. In some countries, especially in the United States, banks became heavily involved in carrying frozen security holdings, which immobilised their resources to a dangerous extent.

In the money market there was a continuous decline of interest rates. Practically every central bank brought its rediscount rate down with a run after the Wall Street slump. To some extent this may have been due to the desire to provide encouragement when such encouragement was badly needed, but the decline was largely due to the absence of demand for funds. Enterprising spirit was at a low ebb, and the decline of commodity prices also reduced the volume of credit required. At the same time, owing to the uncertainty of the outlook, everybody was anxious to keep their resources in a liquid form, and to that end was prepared to be satisfied with a very low yield, or forgo interest altogether. The decline of money rates did not bring about a revival of business activity, for, in the circumstances, cheap money was not sufficient inducement. Already at its early stage, the crisis began to affect the stability of the currencies of some of the agricultural countries, especially in South America. An interesting consequence of the crisis was political instability in a number of countries. It is only human to blame the Government for whatever goes wrong in any country. In countries where the position of the Government was none too stable, the economic crisis brought about violent changes of government and even changes of régime. There were a series of revolutions and *coups d'État* in Latin America and on the Continent. Although other causes may have contributed to many of them, the discontent of the public would not have been aroused to unconstitutional action but for the bad economic conditions.

While the evolution of the crisis was gradual during the first twelve months, it threatened to become rapid at the beginning of its second year. Towards the end of 1930 it appeared as if the crisis would culminate in a panic in more than one country. Early in 1931, however, things began to look brighter, and the improving tendency which became noticeable in several directions aroused hopes that the worst of the crisis was over. There was a slackening in the fall of commodity prices; in fact, in several instances prices registered quite noteworthy recoveries. Retail prices in most countries began to move at last in a downward direction to adjust themselves to wholesale prices. Stock Exchange prices rose, and the wave of banking failures ceased almost completely. In April, however, it was realised that hopes of a recovery were rather premature; there was a relapse in both commodity prices and security prices, and there were a series of failures in various countries, especially in the United States, where, towards the end of April, the atmosphere became almost as alarmist as in December 1930.

The month of May 1931 may be regarded as a turning-point in the crisis. Until then it was reasonable to hope that the world would gradually recover from the depths of depression. The subversive tendencies set in motion by the Creditanstalt crisis have changed, however, the

C

entire aspect of the situation. The difficulties of this
leading bank, which had always been regarded as being
above suspicion, resulted in a wave of distrust against
banks in Central Europe, and caused the wholesale
withdrawal of foreign credits from these banks. In connection with the Creditanstalt affair the conflict between British and French interests led to an open clash,
which disclosed a deplorable lack of co-operation on the
part of France, and accentuated the general pessimism
as to the international outlook. The wholesale withdrawals of foreign funds from Germany, and the simultaneous flight of German capital, assumed in June and
July such dimensions as to threaten the stability of the
reichsmark. Commercial failures of importance in
Germany led to a run on the Darmstädter- und National-
bank, which had to suspend payment on June 13. At
the same time the German Government, in order to
prevent a run on the banks, and the collapse of the
exchange through the withdrawal of foreign credits,
imposed restrictions upon payments by banks which
virtually amounted to a moratorium. These restrictions
were subsequently removed as far as internal payments
were concerned, while German debtors concluded an
agreement with their foreign creditors to postpone the
payment of their short-term liabilities until February
29, 1932.

The German banking crisis has produced tremendous
repercussions all over the world. It resulted in a series
of bank failures in a number of countries, and the im-
mobilisation of German credits caused a wave of distrust which showed itself in the wholesale withdrawal
of foreign funds from London. Foreign banks repatri-
ated their sterling balances in great haste, partly in
order to increase their liquidity in face of the growing

uncertainty, and partly because they were afraid that the German crisis might result in the suspension of the gold standard in Great Britain. Thus the storm centre was shifted from Germany to London. Throughout the summer of 1931 the British authorities made desperate efforts to save sterling, and to that end they concluded foreign credits amounting to £130,000,000. The volume of foreign balances withdrawn was, however, much larger than the resources available. Notwithstanding the efforts to restore confidence by balancing the budget with the aid of drastic fiscal measures, the drain continued, and on September 21 there was no choice but to abandon the gold standard.

The depreciation of sterling after September 21 has considerably aggravated the international crisis. Its immediate effect was to shake the stability of almost every currency, and eventually to compel a number of other countries to suspend the gold standard. For a period in October the storm centre appeared to have shifted from London to New York. The collapse of sterling undermined confidence in the stability of the dollar, and foreign holders of dollar balances hastened to repatriate their funds. This again resulted in a feeling of uneasiness among the American public, and there was a tendency to hoard notes. It was feared that under the dual pressure the Federal Reserve authorities might eventually be compelled to follow the British example in suspending the gold standard. One result of an agreement reached between the French and American authorities was that the former agreed not to withdraw their substantial dollar balances, the drain of foreign funds ceased, and the wave of bank failures caused by the withdrawal of deposits subsided.

In France, too, where the general feeling of uncertainty resulted in a run on a number of banks, and a spectacular increase of hoarding, confidence appeared to have been restored to some extent in November. A number of countries, including Germany and Italy, have successfully resisted the pressure upon their currencies, and have remained on a gold basis. The storm centre appears to have shifted back to London; after a temporary rally in October sterling underwent a violent depreciation in November and December.

The international calamity has been accentuated by the efforts of practically every country to work out its own salvation irrespective of the interests of other countries. A number of Governments have introduced tariffs, or increased the existing ones. Restrictions upon exchanges introduced by various Governments have made it almost impossible to pay for goods bought abroad. Patriotic movements have been initiated in many countries to induce the consumers to buy domestic products. While these tendencies have benefited certain branches of production in every country, they were bound to affect adversely a number of other branches dependent upon exports, and this has contributed to aggravate the economic crisis.

Fortunately, the gloomy anticipations of a general international financial collapse did not materialise. After reaching a low record at 3·23 dollars, sterling underwent a noteworthy recovery. Thanks to the response of the taxpayers to the Government's appeal to their patriotism, the budgetry outlook improved considerably early in January, and this has created a general feeling of optimism. In other countries, too, conditions showed signs of improvement. In France the indemnification of the Bank of France for its losses on its sterling balances has restored confidence in the banks, and hoarding has been checked. Similarly, in the United States the arrangements made for the support of banks in difficulties has reassured public opinion and has put an end to the wholesale failure of banks. The conclusion of a standstill agreement for twelve months with Germany has eliminated an important source of uncertainty. The repayment of the Franco-American credits contracted in the defence of sterling during 1931 has restored confidence in sterling, and the spectacular recovery of London's position has revived hopes that before very long Great Britain would be in a position to give a lead in international reconstruction.

Unfortunately, this optimism was, to say the least of it, premature. The efforts of the American authorities to check the fall of commodity prices by pursuing a "reflationist" monetary policy were of no avail. The prices of most commodities continued to decline, while stock exchange quotations declined to new low records. Although the banking situation was on the whole more stable than during the second half of 1931, there were isolated failures and liquidations of importance in various parts of the world. The collapse of the Kreuger and Toll group, and the astounding revelations as to the fraudulent basis of its activities, have dealt a severe blow upon confidence. It has inflicted heavy losses upon almost every country, in particular upon Sweden, Switzerland, France, and the United States. It was feared that this new crisis would result in a general relapse. Although the atmosphere was decidedly dangerous for some weeks in more than one financial centre, the adverse rumours that came into circulation as to the effect of the crisis upon a number of banks were unable to provoke panic.

At the time of writing it is impossible to say whether

the climax has been passed. A great deal depends upon
the possibility of arriving at some understanding with
regard to Reparations and German debts. It is feared
that failure of the efforts to reach an agreement may
result in political and economic chaos in Germany,
which again would cause disastrous losses to her
creditor countries. The fear of such developments is
weighing like a nightmare on the minds of mankind,
and is regarded as the principal obstacle to recovery.
In this respect, the situation has improved as a
result of the Lausanne Agreement; but uncertainty
continues to prevail about the willingness of the
United States to waive war debts, without which the
results of Lausanne would become illusory.

PART II

CAUSES OF THE CRISIS

CHAPTER III

EXPLANATIONS OF THE CRISIS

IT is a commonplace of economic text-books that the function of economic science is to explain and foresee economic phenomena. The view is widely held that, in the case of the present world economic crisis, economic science has failed deplorably to fulfil its task. This conception does, however, rather less than justice to the exponents of economic science of our generation. It is true that few economists, if any, were aware of the coming trouble, and that, even after its arrival, they were unable to gauge its significance, or to provide an adequate explanation. The uninitiated public complains—and not altogether without reason—of having been left in the dark as to the causes of the world-wide depression. Many attempts have been made to provide the much-needed explanation, but none of them carry much conviction. The main reason for this is that most attempts aiming at the explanation of the crisis are partisan, either because those who put them forward strive to establish or support a theory of their own or because they are too eager to use the facts of the crisis to defend or attack certain political or economic interests.

At the same time, it is beyond question that many of the theories put forward contain a certain percentage of truth; in spite of their one-sidedness, they undoubtedly contribute towards finding the right solution. It is obvious that the present economic crisis is the outcome of the combination of a large number of causes. Those economists who are inclined to overemphasise one single cause in which they are particularly interested may not provide the complete explanation, but certainly contribute towards it. After all, exaggeration is sometimes necessary to draw attention to certain facts which may be overlooked unless they become the subject of controversy.

In examining the causes of the crisis, it is necessary to discriminate between the set of causes to which the depression of November 1929–May 1931 is attributed, and the set of causes which are regarded as responsible for the accentuation of the crisis into a financial panic during the second half of 1931. In this part of the book we shall confine ourselves to the enumeration of the causes of the economic crisis, while the financial crisis will be examined in Chapter XIV.

We propose to enumerate below the principal theories which have been put forward to explain the earlier stages of the present crisis, and to examine them, one by one, in subsequent chapters.

(1) Periodic crises (business cycles).
(2) The necessity to return to the pre-war level.
(3) Overproduction.
(4) Underconsumption.
(5) Monetary causes.
(6) Overcapitalisation.
(7) Overspeculation.
(8) The moral factor.
(9) Coincidence of a number of independent factors.

(1) According to an explanation popular with the

pre-war school of economists, there is nothing exceptional or extraordinary in the present crisis. Before the
war, there was a crisis on the average every seven or
eight years, and nothing that has happened since
1914 has changed this state of affairs. Although the
war disorganised economic life throughout the world,
it made no difference in the fundamental tendencies
which have been responsible for the crises since the
beginning of the modern economic system. But for
the war, the crisis would most probably have occurred
about 1917; as a result of exceptional circumstances,
it was postponed till 1920. In less than ten years the
business cycle ran its course once more and, after the
period of comparative stability and prosperity, produced the crisis that broke loose in 1929.

(2) A section of the representatives of economic
thought has always held the opinion that normal conditions could not be regarded as having been attained
until the world price level had declined to its pre-war
figure. A very large section of the public held the same
opinion. Those who remember pre-war conditions
would find it difficult to regard any conditions other
than those as normal and permanent. During the
period of comparative stability between 1922 and 1928
many people were inclined to hold the view that equilibrium had been attained at a price level which was
different from the pre-war level. They argued that
economic conditions had changed considerably since
the war, and that, even if there had been no war at
all, the price level would have probably moved in an
upward direction. They failed to convince, however,
a large section of both expert and public opinion, who
regard the fall of prices as the justification of their belief
in the necessity for the return to pre-war prices.

(3) As the immediate cause of the decline of prices was the accumulation of stocks in various branches of production, a natural conclusion is that we are faced with the phenomenon of overproduction. There is no doubt about it that both agricultural and industrial production have increased considerably during the last few years and, in many branches, is in excess of its pre-war figures. The world is suffering, therefore, from acute *embarras de richesse*.

(4) Those who are not satisfied with the superficial explanation of the crisis as a result of the increase of production arrive at the conclusion that the reason why the surplus cannot be absorbed is deficient consumption. It stands to reason that, if the world produces more, its inhabitants should be better off and not worse off than they were before. If this is not the case, there must be something which prevents them from consuming the goods they produce. A great variety of theories are put forward to explain this phenomenon of underconsumption. According to some, the habit of saving is responsible for it; according to another, disequilibrium between the production of capital goods and consumers' goods is the source of the evil.

(5) One of the most popular explanations of the crisis is that the depression and the fall of prices are due to monetary causes. The maldistribution of gold is regarded by many of our leading economists as the root of all evil. It is said that although the world's gold stock available for monetary purposes is larger than before the war, the major part of it is hoarded in two countries, while the rest of the world does not possess an adequate supply to meet its monetary requirements. As a result, the volume of currency and credit based on the gold stock is not sufficient

to enable the consumers to buy all the goods that are produced.

(6) The excessive amount of fictitious wealth as represented by the enormous increase of public and private indebtedness in every country is regarded as one of the causes of the present crisis. The productive section of the population in every country has to carry an unbearable burden of deadweight debt in the form of excessive taxation. Relief from these burdens can come either through the depreciation of currencies (which would cause a substantial rise in the prices of the commodities or manufactured goods produced by the debtors) or else through the repudiation of the debts themselves.

(7) In the past most crises were preceded by a frenzy of speculation. As the present crisis was preceded by the Wall Street boom, it is natural that there should be people who should regard overspeculation as the cause which led to the crisis.

(8) According to another explanation, the crisis was due to the lack of confidence on the part of the public, brought about by a series of disappointments suffered during the last few years. In almost every country there have been a number of financial frauds and scandals of great magnitude, and millions of investors suffered heavy losses in consequence. It is not surprising, therefore, that the public become distrustful and adopt for a time a reserved attitude.

(9) An essentially practical explanation is that the world crisis is the outcome of the coincidence of a number of independent factors, such as the untimely increase of wheat production brought about by the increasing use of tractors, the demonetisation of silver, the suspension of American foreign lending, and, last

but not least, Soviet activities. According to this theory, all these factors were completely independent of each other. In themselves they would not have caused much damage, but owing to the unfortunate fact that they happened to coincide, their combined effect was responsible for the crisis.

Our task is to examine how far the causes given by these various theories may have contributed to bring about the crisis. The contradiction between the explanations is more apparent than real; each of them contains some constructive elements which are well worth retaining.

CHAPTER IV

THE "BUSINESS CYCLES" THEORY

FOR the last century or so our best economic brains have been puzzled by the causes which are responsible for the business cycle, which has repeated itself over and over again in the course of the nineteenth century. Every ten years or so there was a crisis, followed by a prolonged period of economic depression. After a while, a process of recovery began to set in; it was slow at first, but, as it progressed, it became more and more accentuated and culminated in a wave of prosperity and a speculative boom. This again was followed by a more or less spectacular crash to conclude the cycle. We do not propose to deal here with all the theories which have been put forward to explain this phenomenon. Some economists went so far as to accuse the spots on the sun or the fluctuations of the barometer of being responsible for these cycles. The common-sense explanation is that which attributes the crises to excessive optimism and pessimism. It is in accordance with human nature that, when conditions are fairly satisfactory, the public should take it for granted that such conditions would last for ever. If business is moderately profitable, everybody is inclined to think that it will always remain so. For this reason people are tempted to anticipate further profits in their plans of production and consumption. Producers are induced to extend their plants, consumers are inclined to spend beyond the limits of their actual means, in the hope of a gradual increase of their earnings. Speculators take it for granted that the conditions of rising commodity and security prices would go on indefinitely, and they are inclined to discount further appreciations. Hence the stock exchange booms which usually accompany periods of prosperity.

Up to a point optimism is undoubtedly justified, for, in spite of all set-backs, mankind has made progress during the past century or so. It is when anticipations become exaggerated that they become dangerous. A stage is reached when the position loses touch with reality, and at this stage a comparatively moderate blow is sufficient to bring about the collapse of the house of cards thus built. A short crop, or even an excessively good crop, a local crisis in some branch of production, a business failure of importance brought about by purely local causes, and a good many other factors—any one of them is sufficient to prick the bubble and cause a sharp crisis. A slump in security prices is usually the first manifestation of the crisis ; it is usually followed by a slump of commodity prices and a prolonged period of general depression. If excessive optimism was largely responsible for the speculative boom which brought about the crisis, so excessive pessimism is responsible for the violence of the crisis and the delay in recovery.

Let us examine how far this factor was responsible for the present crisis. Those who maintain that the crisis of 1929–1931 is the repetition of the classical pre-war crisis are inclined to overlook the fact that, generally speaking, the present crisis was not preceded by a speculative boom. Although there had been excessive speculation in Wall Street, and the United States experienced an unprecedented period of prosperity, there had been little trace of either prosperity or boom in most other parts of the world. Conditions in Europe can hardly be said to have been prosperous previous to the Wall Street collapse at the end of 1929. Many countries, including Great Britain, suffered from acute economic depression, while even in countries which were comparatively prosperous, such as France, for instance, there was no trace of any speculative boom which would have justified a collapse. It is possible, of course, that the United States has acquired such enormous influence over the economic life of the world that the situation in that country is capable of governing world economic currents. To that extent it is correct to say that the crisis was the culmination of the business cycle as it was known in pre-war days. For the United States provided, unquestionably, a classical example of over-speculation and excessive optimism which was bound to lead to a crisis.

There were, admittedly, certain symptoms also in other countries which might have played a certain part in preparing the ground for the crisis. In Great Britain, for instance, though there had been no general economic boom, there was in 1928 and 1929 a promoting boom in companies of certain special types. Possibly a general economic boom, such as was witnessed in the United States, was prevented by factors particular to Great Britain. As this country depends to a great extent upon a few branches of industries which, for particular reasons, were anything but prosperous, the wave of prosperity was unable to spread

D

here. In Germany again, it was the special conditions created by the problem of Reparations, and by the destruction of savings by inflation, that prevented the development of a wave of prosperity. Most other continental countries were undergoing a process of readjustment as a result of the recent stabilisation of their currencies, so that economic tendencies were prevented from taking their normal course.

In most countries outside Europe, too, abnormal local conditions prevented the operation of the factors which worked normally in the United States. In Japan, for instance, the speculative activity that followed the earthquake reconstruction had collapsed already in 1927, so that, at the time of the American boom, that country was just emerging from a state of depression. The South American states had to struggle with their exchange problems, but to some extent the American wave of prosperity extended also to them as a result of the loans which were freely granted to them by the United States. The country which experienced the same phenomena as the United States, though to a more moderate extent, was Canada, which is economically closely connected with the United States.

It cannot be said that the anticipation of a collapse as a result of excessive speculation played a great part in bringing about the crisis. On the contrary, a good many people were inclined to think that conditions are now different from pre-war conditions, and that the phenomena which repeated themselves with unmerciful regularity before the war need not ever repeat themselves again. It was thanks to this belief that the wave of prosperity and the speculative boom in the United States could assume such unprecedented dimensions.

Although, generally speaking, the history of the present crisis does not exactly correspond to the classical rules of a crisis, at the same time it is obvious that those rules are still in existence, even though their working may be modified by individual conditions in individual countries to a far greater extent than before the war. After all, human nature has not been fundamentally changed by the war. If in pre-war days steady prosperity, or even the absence of any serious disturbing factor, tended to create excessive optimism in the public mind, there is no reason why the same circumstances should not tend to have exactly the same effect in our days. It is, therefore, certain that the fundamental tendency which has characterised modern economic life, that periods of prosperity should be followed by crisis and depression, is still in existence and played an important part in bringing about the crisis of 1929-1931.

In arriving at this conclusion we do not claim, however, to have provided the explanation of the crisis. In addition to the tendencies responsible for the working of the business cycle, there are a number of other factors which played a considerable part in bringing about the crisis and which have no direct connection with the tendencies which account for the repetition of the classical periodical crisis. We do not propose to examine in detail the causes of the periodical crisis, for it would require volumes. The problem has an immense literature, and there is little or nothing to be said which has not been said before. Let us confine ourselves to the simple explanation of this type of crisis by the psychological factor of excessive optimism and pessimism. The other factors which, in addition to the tendencies to a periodical crisis, were responsible for our present troubles, will be dealt with in subsequent chapters. It is necessary to point out here, however, that although they may be technically independent of the fundamental factor tending to bring about a periodical crisis, in reality they may perhaps also be regarded as part of the process. After all, there is usually an outside influence which brings about the collapse of the boom, and from this point of view the difference between the present crisis and pre-war crises may be merely one of degree, not of kind.

In accepting the view that the operation of the system of business cycles played an important part in bringing about the present crisis, we do not necessarily adhere to the economic fatalism which regards such a crisis as inevitable. Possibly the present crisis could have been prevented had the authorities of various countries, especially of the United States, been better prepared for it, and had there been a closer co-operation between various economic interests within a country and between the authorities of the various countries. In the last part of this book an attempt will be made to suggest ways by which the periodical crisis could in future be eliminated or mitigated. It is to be hoped that the present crisis will provide a useful lesson to prove the necessity for closer co-operation in every sphere of economic life.

CHAPTER V

IT has become a general habit since the war to look
back upon pre-war days as upon a kind of lost paradise,
and to regard the endeavour to return to pre-war conditions as the sacred duty of this generation. Com-
paring the experience of the pre-war years with that of
early post-war years, it is only natural that pre-war
conditions should be regarded as ideal and their many
shortcomings forgotten by comparison with the miseries
caused by the war. This desire to return to comfortable
pre-war conditions was particularly deeply rooted in
the minds of the public as far as the price level was
concerned. Those who still remember pre-war conditions cannot help feeling that those were happier days
when prices were much lower. It is true that the
earnings of most people have duly adjusted themselves
to post-war conditions, so that most of them can afford
to pay the present higher prices as easily as, or more
easily than, they could pay the lower prices before the
war. All that has happened is that we have to calculate
with larger figures. There are, however, a fairly large
number of people whose incomes did not keep pace
with the rise in prices, and who have, therefore, a legitimate grievance against the post-war price level. But
if the question whether prices and incomes should
return to pre-war level were to be decided by plebis-

cite, there is no doubt that the result would be against the restoration of pre-war conditions. At the same time, there is, needless to say, a desire on the part of everybody to obtain a decline of the price level without having to consent to a decline of their own incomes.

The desire for a return to the pre-war price level by a large section of public opinion would not, in itself, have been sufficient to bring about a decline of prices, but psychologically it prepared the ground for such a movement; although the school of thought which believed that any price level higher than the pre-war level was necessarily temporary, and that no permanent stability could be attained unless the pre-war level is restored, was subjected to much criticism, their theory certainly contained a great deal of truth. The idea was much more popular among the general public and practical business men than among theoretical economists. The psychological factor was decidedly favourable to a decline of prices, and was undoubtedly responsible for the accentuation of the decline, since it was brought about by material factors. The idea that it was an inevitable necessity to return to the pre-war level was inspired by the same economic fatalism as the theory according to which the repetition of the periodical crisis was inevitable. For a return to the pre-war price level, necessitating a decline from the 1929 level of about 40 per cent, could not be imagined without a violent crisis, or at least a prolonged period of depression, according to whether the decline was to take place suddenly or gradually. A decline in prices has always been accompanied by a crisis and depression, just as a rise in prices has usually been accompanied by real or fictitious prosperity.

Although in theory an all-round change of prices would make no difference so long as incomes and the cost of living adjust themselves to the new level, in practice a falling price level invariably results in a depression and a crisis. The crisis, on the other hand, tends to accentuate the fall of prices because of its paralysing effect upon the demand for commodities.

It is evident, therefore, that those who anticipated a return to pre-war prices held the opinion, consciously or unconsciously, that a crisis was inevitable. Their opinion may have helped, to some extent, to accentuate the depression, just as the opinion of those who believe that the periodical crisis is inevitable have contributed to such crises. The difference between the two kinds of economic fatalism is that while the believers in periodical crises will expect another crisis in about seven or eight years' time, the believers in a return to pre-war conditions are now more or less satisfied. As we have practically reached the pre-war level, all that is needed is that everything should be adjusted to the new level of wholesale prices and normal conditions are restored. In their opinion, once this has been attained, there is no need to anticipate any further crises. Thus, while at the beginning of the downward movement they were pessimistic, they have grown gradually more and more optimistic the nearer we get to the pre-war level. Their optimism will increase when retail prices have adjusted themselves to wholesale prices, and this will provide a psychological factor which will contribute to the revival.

There is no doubt that the discrepancy between wholesale and retail prices, which developed in consequence of the sharp decline of the former, has a large share in the responsibility for the accentuation of the depression. When the fall of the wholesale prices became a matter of general knowledge, everybody expected that retail prices would follow. The decline of retail prices, however, is necessarily a very slow process. It may take many months and perhaps even several years before the level of retail prices has adjusted itself to the level of wholesale prices. Meanwhile the consumers, expecting a fall of retail prices, abstained as far as possible from buying beyond the absolute necessities. Against this natural attitude it was useless to advocate an increase of spending in order to relieve the crisis.

From the point of view of the adjustment of retail prices to the new level of wholesale prices it is, therefore, undoubtedly true that normal conditions cannot return until the process of readjustment has been completed. The believers in the pre-war level are right, therefore, as far as the adjustment of retail prices is concerned.

CHAPTER VI

IN dealing with the question of overproduction, it is necessary to discriminate between absolute and relative overproduction. The former means that the total goods produced are in excess of the requirements of the consumers; the latter means that the output in certain branches of production, or at a certain price, is in excess of requirements. Theoretically, absolute overproduction is impossible, for there is no limit to the wants of mankind. It is true that there are certain limits beyond which the increase of the production of foodstuffs and a number of other articles for consumption becomes superfluous, but for an immense variety of goods the saturation point is at such a distance as to justify regarding it as non-existent in practice. Possibly, if a stage is attained when every single human being is housed in a palace and is surrounded with every comfort and luxury, a further increase of production becomes superfluous; but it is sufficient to remember the highly unsatisfactory living conditions of the predominant majority of mankind to realise how far we are from this happy state of affairs. What most people regard as overproduction is usually a case of underconsumption. This means that the total amount of goods produced is by no means in excess of the needs of mankind, but is in excess of the amount they are

41

able or willing to buy. While it is thus unreasonable to talk about absolute overproduction as the cause of the present crisis, there is not the least doubt that relative overproduction occupies a prominent place among its causes.

There has been unquestionably a tendency in the world, since the war, to increase production. This was, at the beginning of the post-war period, a reaction to the exceptional war conditions which resulted in a wasteful use and a consequent shortage of most kinds of commodities. Both industry and agriculture were anxious to produce more in order to satisfy the increased demand and to replenish stocks depleted during the war. This movement soon came to a climax in 1920, and was followed by a temporary reaction during the following two years. A factor which had a more lasting effect upon production was the increase of economic nationalism since the war. As a result of the difficulties experienced during the war in obtaining goods produced in other countries, there has been a tendency in practically every country to become more self-supporting. Agricultural countries considered it desirable to build up new branches of industries, while industrial countries felt it their duty to attempt to increase their local production of food and raw material. The changes of political frontiers have also contributed to accentuate this tendency. Every political unit created by the Peace Treaty endeavoured to be as self-supporting as the whole unit had formerly been of which it formed a part before the war.

The industrialisation of agricultural countries was a much easier task than the increase of the production of raw material and food in industrial countries. In every agricultural country, from China to Peru, a large

number of factories were erected during and after the
war under the protection of customs tariffs. Those
responsible for this policy of industrialisation believed
that it would lead to a new era of unequalled prosperity. While agriculture provided them only with
their bare necessities, they hoped that the additional
national revenue created by this process of industrialisation would provide a great many luxuries. They overlooked the fact that in reducing their purchases from
the industrial countries which supplied them with manufactures before the war, they reduced the capacity
of those countries to buy agricultural products. For
some years the effect of this tendency upon the demand
for agricultural products did not make itself felt. After
all, agricultural products are needed to satisfy primary
necessities, and the demand for them is not affected to
a very great extent by a condition of depression in
industrial countries. It was only when industrial
countries had decided to follow the example of agricultural countries in making themselves more self-
supporting that the reaction of the short-sighted policy
of agricultural countries began to make itself felt. It
took several years before this policy began to produce
practical results. In several countries, notably Great
Britain, the endeavour to increase agricultural production has, so far, remained only a dream supported
by a section of the public; but in other countries,
especially in Italy and to a lesser extent in Germany,
it has become an actual fact. The "Grain Battle", as
the movement was popularly called in Italy, resulted
in a considerable decline of Italian demand for foreign
agricultural products. Thus the increased industrialisation of agricultural countries did not benefit their
population, as they find it now increasingly difficult to

market their agricultural products. All that has happened is that in many countries both manufactures and agricultural products are now produced under less favourable conditions than they were before the war.

Another factor which tended to bring about over-production in certain branches is the system of restrictions and artificial prices introduced after the war. In several branches of production in which a certain country or a certain group of producers had a practical monopoly, attempts have been made to keep up the price of the product at an artificial level by means of restrictions imposed on production or on export. The most characteristic example of such experiments was the rubber restriction introduced by British rubber producers. Its result was to maintain the price of rubber for several years at a price that was highly profitable to producers, and, consequently, rubber production increased to a very great extent in countries which did not fall in with the scheme of restriction. Another characteristic example was that of coffee valorisation. The Brazilian authorities, by means of restricting the export of coffee, and by means of financing the accumulation of stocks, succeeded for several years in maintaining the price of coffee at an artificially high level. In consequence there has been a substantial increase of production in all coffee-producing countries. The system did not confine itself to agriculture. In the mining industry it has also been attempted to keep prices at an artificially high level with similar consequences to those noticed in agriculture; obvious examples are tin and copper.

Technical improvements were also largely responsible for the increase of production, especially as far as agriculture is concerned, for, with the aid of the use of machinery, it has become possible to increase the production of grain to a very great extent. In industry too, technical improvements have increased the producing capacity of plants.

In practically every branch of production there has been either an actual increase of output or else a potential increase of capacity. In an ideal world this should not and could not be a cause of crisis; if everybody produces more, everybody should consume more, and the increase of production should have for result an increased prosperity. It is possible to imagine that, if only part of mankind were to increase their production, they could not benefit by it unless the rest of mankind followed their example, but it is more difficult to understand why everybody has not benefited by an all-round increase. Thus, while it is evident that the increase of production has contributed to a very great extent to the crisis, it cannot, in itself, be regarded as an explanation. There must be causes why this increase of production did not have for effect a corresponding increase of consumption. The chapters dealing with the questions of underconsumption and of the disturbed equilibrium will attempt to provide the explanation.

CHAPTER VII

UNDERCONSUMPTION

WE have said in the previous chapter that there can be no general overproduction in the real sense of the term. There may be disequilibrium between various branches of production, or there may be under-consumption for a great variety of reasons. The total amount of goods produced can exceed the volume that people can buy, but not the volume that they need. In most cases, when people talk about over-production we are confronted with the phenomenon of underconsumption. This means that the consumers do not buy all the goods that are produced, either because they deliberately abstain from buying, or else because they do not possess the necessary means for buying them. Before the war, several explanations of recurring economic crises were based on the assumption that the habit of saving was the root of all evil. As the total amount earned by producers is not spent, the economists said, part of the goods produced is not bought. This theory, however, seems to overlook the fact that considerable sections of the population in every country do not do any actual producing work, but possess nevertheless the purchasing power to buy part of the goods produced by the productive section of the population.

The theory according to which the crisis is due to

inadequate wages has the same weakness. Although it is true that there would be a greater demand for certain types of goods if wages were to represent a larger proportion of the total national income, on the other hand this would make it impossible to spend a sufficient amount on other types of goods. There is a theory of more recent origin, according to which our troubles are due to disequilibrium between production of capital goods and consumption goods. According to this theory, an excessively large proportion of the world's financial resources is devoted to the creation of capital goods, as a result of which productive capacity increases, while the demand for consumption goods decreases. Although this theory is in itself inadequate to explain the crisis, it is certainly more convincing than the primitive theories attempting to place the responsibility for the crisis either upon excess of saving or upon inadequacy of wages.

As in the case of overproduction, so in the case of underconsumption, it is necessary to discriminate between absolute and relative underconsumption, according to whether the total demand for goods is less than the volume produced, or whether the demand for particular categories of goods is smaller than the output. There can be little doubt that the total demand for goods, far from having declined, has undergone a considerable increase since the war. As a result of the increase in the real wages of the working classes, in most countries, the consuming power of the population has tended to increase. Moreover, in many former belligerent countries, the rural population acquired new habits and tastes in a period of relative prosperity during, and immediately after, the war. In countries outside Europe the population has begun to develop

a demand for modern manufactures. The shortage of
housing accommodation, which became very acute just
after the war, and which in many countries has not
yet been satisfied, is due not so much to the destruction of property during the war or the postponement
of building activities, as to the increased requirements
of the population for better housing accommodation.

Another factor responsible for the increase of consumption after the war is the popularisation of the
system of instalment buying. It is especially in the
United States that the system has shown such spectacular development during the last few years, but it
has been adopted also in other countries. As a result
there has been a remarkable increase in the demand
for goods. The salaried classes and a great many wage-
earners, in addition to spending their current incomes,
tend to acquire the habit of spending a very considerable portion of their future incomes. In many
respects this system was beginning to go beyond
normal proportions, and created overconsumption.
After the beginning of the crisis an immediate reaction set in. As many wage-earners became unemployed in every country, and many more regarded
their future employment as uncertain, instalment buying declined considerably. Apart from this, as hundreds
of thousands of people pledged their salaries in advance, they acquired all they wanted months ahead,
so that there was bound to be a natural decline in their
demand. Although the decline of demand on that
account was decidedly a case of underconsumption, it
ought to be regarded as an effect of the crisis rather
than the cause. It has, of course, contributed to the
accentuation of the crisis and to the postponement of
recovery.

While general underconsumption cannot be regarded, therefore, as having been responsible for provoking the crisis, there has been undoubtedly special underconsumption in more than one direction. In the first place, to some extent there was underconsumption on the part of the debtor countries of Europe. Germany, and to a lesser extent the Allied countries with war debts to the United States, had to use part of their national income in payment of interest and sinking fund on these debts. If this necessity had not existed, these amounts would have been available for a corresponding increase of consumption. Other cases of underconsumption occurred in silver-using countries. As a result of the depreciation of silver during the last few years, the purchasing power of China, India, and other Eastern countries has been severely reduced. The price of silver declined from 36d. an ounce in 1924 to about 12d. an ounce in 1931, as a result of which the purchasing power of half the world's population has been greatly reduced. Although the requirements of the inhabitants of the countries affected are few, the enormous size of the population represents a considerable factor in world consumption, and the reduction of their purchasing power cannot help but affect the total demand for goods.

The sudden reduction of American lending abroad, especially to Central Europe and Latin America, was also one of the causes of relative underconsumption. The freedom with which the United States granted loans to Latin American countries and to Germany during the period 1924–1928 was largely responsible for the atmosphere of fictitious prosperity created in those countries. As a result of the Wall Street boom, lending abroad was drastically reduced during 1928

E

and 1929. As the amounts lent in previous years were spent on the creation of capital goods, all that was left was the necessity of paying interest on them. Being unable to receive fresh loans, the countries concerned had to curtail their purchases.

Apart from these causes, there has been local under-consumption in various countries and in various sections of the population as a result of the changes that have taken place since the war.

CHAPTER VIII

THE MONETARY FACTOR

THOSE who held the view that prices were bound to go down to their pre-war level had one powerful argument with which to support their theory. They maintained that the supply of monetary gold was inadequate to cover the requirement of the world on the basis of a price level which was about 40 per cent above the pre-war figure. For, although the gold stocks available for monetary purposes were considerably higher in 1929 than in 1913, a large part of this stock was hoarded in a few countries, notably the United States and France. The stock available for the remaining nations of the world was, therefore, inadequate to cover their requirements. It ought to be remembered that, during the period between 1925 and 1929, a larger number of countries established a gold standard than during the whole of the nineteenth century. Most of them did not possess sufficient gold to cover their note circulation, and they entered the market as buyers rather than sellers of gold. Apart from the two countries mentioned, and a few other countries, such as the Argentine and Spain, most countries possessed only very narrow margins of gold reserves above their legal minimum requirements. They were, therefore, sensitive to any influence which tended to reduce the gold supply available for them.

In face of an inadequate supply of gold, caused largely by the maldistribution of the existing stock, the monetary authorities had to meet abnormal factors which resulted from time to time in strong pressure upon their gold reserves. The increase of the international short-term indebtedness after the war has been the source of large international transfers of funds, actual and potential, which in themselves would have made it necessary to keep an unusually large margin of gold reserves. For a variety of considerations capital has become much more restless than before the war, and the volume of international transfers on capital account was many times its pre-war figure. Thus the higher price level was not the only factor that increased the requirements of gold.

These were the conditions which, as a result of French gold demand, assumed exceptional importance from a general economic point of view. Although the amount withdrawn by France during the last three years is a small part of the total gold stock of the world, it is considerable as compared with the amount left after the deduction of the gold supply of the United States and France. The proportion to which the withdrawal of gold on French account tended to reduce the basis of currency and credit for the rest of the world was, therefore, by no means inconsiderable.

In the opinion of several leading experts, this factor was, more than any other single factor, responsible for the origin of the crisis. Although such views may be exaggerated and one-sided, there can be no doubt that the French gold demand played a considerable part in bringing about the fall of prices, not merely through its direct effect on the monetary situation but also through its subtle psychological influence. It may

be argued that no actual deflation took place during
1929; it is certain, however, that the French demand
for gold was largely responsible for preventing Great
Britain and other countries from expanding their credit
to a sufficient extent to replace the funds attracted
from Europe to Wall Street. For, unfortunately, the
French demand for gold coincided with a wholesale flow
of capital from London and other European centres to
New York, as a result of the Wall Street boom. In
consequence of this movement, the margin of the gold
reserves in Great Britain and several continental
countries tended to narrow down further. But for the
French withdrawal of gold from London, this market
would have been in a position to replace to some extent
the funds withdrawn, not only from this country, but
also from other countries. As a result of the dual pressure, however, London was unable to fulfil this function.
It may be said, therefore, that the all-round increase
of bank rates in Europe during 1929 was due at least
to the same extent to the French demand for gold as
to the reckless speculation in Wall Street.

The opinion is widely held that the French authorities cannot be exonerated from the blame of pursuing a
monetary policy which tended to aggravate the situation at a time when it was of great importance to
counteract the disturbing factor of the Wall Street
boom. Even if we were to accept the argument of the
apologists for the French authorities, that the French
gold withdrawals were not the result of a gold policy
but of the absence of a gold policy, this cannot be
regarded as an excuse. After all, it is the duty of the
authorities of any country to pursue a constructive
policy and not merely to abstain from interfering with
the working of destructive factors.

An increase of bank rate always tends to bring about a decline of prices. There is no reason to suppose that during 1929 this was not the case. The decline of commodity prices began, in fact, towards the middle of 1929, several months before the Wall Street slump. Although the collapse in October 1929 accentuated the decline of commodity prices, it cannot be regarded as the immediate cause of that tendency. The increase of bank rates necessitated largely by the French gold policy was mainly responsible for the downward trend of prices, and was, therefore, one of the immediate causes leading to the world crisis.

The psychological effect of the French gold policy was also one of the factors tending to bring about the crisis. The lack of co-operation between the principal countries was becoming increasingly evident in the course of 1929. It was calculated to inspire distrust and pessimism and accentuated the collapse.

If the French authorities had a large share in the responsibility for bringing about the crisis, their responsibility for the accentuation and prolongation of the crisis is even more obvious. During 1930, when the crisis was in full swing, they continued their policy to a disquieting extent. Even in the autumn of 1930, when the position was becoming increasingly dangerous, they failed to realise the necessity for co-operating to the common good. At a time when the world appeared to be on the verge of the greatest financial disaster of modern times, and when the least cause would have been sufficient to bring about a world-wide panic, they continued to play with fire right over the powder-magazine. In November and December 1930 there was a serious run on banks, both in the United States and in France. Both French and American banks called in their credits recklessly from their foreign customers; but for the support received from London banks, there would have been a wholesale failure of banks, commercial and industrial firms all over the world. Even at this moment, when London appeared to remain the only fixed point and the only steadying influence, the French authorities continued to pursue a policy which was indirectly responsible for the withdrawal of gold from London, thereby endangering the stability of this market. Had the wave of distrust, which did not spare even the leading banks in New York and Paris, spread to London, the international financial disaster would have occurred in 1930 instead of 1931. London stood, however, this test remarkably well, and after the turn of the year conditions appeared to be somewhat calmer. It was only then that the French authorities showed some willingness to adopt a policy of co-operation, which has unquestionably contributed towards the increase of confidence. Had the improvement of financial relations between London and Paris proved to be of a lasting character, it might have averted the banking crisis of July 1931, and possibly we should be, by now, well on our way towards recovery.

CHAPTER IX

DISTURBED EQUILIBRIUM

WE have seen in previous chapters that, for a great variety of causes, a series of changes have taken place during the last few years, both in production and consumption. It is a well-known fact that whenever the smooth working of our economic system is disturbed, for whatever reason it may be, the immediate consequence is that some sections of producers and consumers are bound to suffer. Even though the disturbance involves a change for the better, the immediate effect upon a certain number of people is usually unfavourable. Economic history has innumerable examples to prove this. The construction of railways ruined the coaches and the canals, and reduced thousands of people to poverty. The progress of manufacturing industries means ruin for large classes of craftsmen who, in many branches of manufacture, cannot compete either in quality or in price with the factory-produced goods. It is beyond dispute that the abolition of customs tariffs all over the world would be desirable and would result in immense improvement. Its immediate effect would be, however, to throw out of work a number of industrial enterprises. Thousands of factory hands would become unemployed, thousands of farmers would be ruined. Undoubtedly the unemployed would gradually be absorbed by the

increased activities of those branches of production
in every country which, under the new conditions of
free trade, proved to be the most efficient. It might,
however, take a generation to overcome the immediate
effects of the sudden change. Thus, even if the changes
are, on balance, beneficial to mankind, their effect
during the transition period may be disadvantageous
to particular interests and even to mankind as a whole.
A characteristic example of the adverse effect of such
favourable changes is provided by the present agricultural crisis, which is largely the consequence of the improvement of agricultural methods and the reduction
of the costs of production. Another, even more obvious,
example is the effect of rationalisation upon unemployment.

If the changes in the working of our economic system
are for the worse, then equilibrium is upset to at least
the same extent as in the case of favourable changes,
without the compensation of ultimate benefit. Since
the war, a large number of such changes have taken
place in every sphere of economic activity. As we
pointed out in a previous chapter, a number of agricultural countries became partially industrialised, in spite
of the less favourable conditions in which they could
produce manufactures; while some primarily industrial
countries have diverted much of their energy to increasing their agricultural production. In every country,
certain interests may have benefited by the change,
but other interests had to suffer. The buying capacity
of certain classes may have increased, but that of others
has declined as a result of the change. The repeated
increases of customs barriers, which have taken place
in almost every country, have had a similar effect.

The changes brought about by the war in the dis-

tribution of wealth, both within a single country and
as between various countries, have also constituted
changes fraught with unfavourable consequences.
Every country witnessed the impoverishment of important classes; although the loss of their purchasing
power was compensated by the increase in the purchasing power of other classes, a change has, nevertheless, disturbed equilibrium. Similarly, the impoverishment of Europe and the simultaneous accumulation
of wealth in the United States was also bound to
affect economic equilibrium.

It is true that, in several instances, post-war changes
have produced an immediate beneficial effect. New
branches of production have been created, and they
provide employment and profit for a number of people.
For instance, the manufacturing of wireless, artificial
silk, etc., has made up to some extent for the decline
in the demand for other manufactures. But those who
benefited by this were not necessarily the same people
who suffered as a result of the decline in the demand
for other kinds of goods.

Had the changes been gradual, their effect would
have been less pronounced; but a great number of important changes took place in the course of a very few
years, and their coincidence accentuated their adverse
effect upon economic equilibrium. It ought to be borne
in mind that various branches of production and consumption in various countries are, nowadays, very
closely inter-related, so that depression in one branch
is bound to affect other branches of industry in the
same country and production as a whole in other
countries. Had there been closer co-operation between
various economic interests, it might have been possible
to moderate the adverse effect of changes. In our

present circumstances, however, people bring about changes, regardless of their indirect consequences, which, in a great many cases, react upon those responsible for the changes. In this way also the disturbance of economic equilibrium was largely due to inadequate co-operation between various economic interests and between nations.

CHAPTER X

THE MORAL FACTOR

WE live in the age of statistics, when the economic situation, the development of the crisis, and the chances of recovery are expressed in terms of index numbers, figures of commodity stocks, car loadings, unfilled orders, and the like. Doubtless these figures convey a great deal of information to the select few who are in a position to interpret them intelligently. They only present, however, part of the picture. There are factors and tendencies which cannot be expressed in terms of figures, and the working of which is too intangible to be measured statistically. The effect of the same material factors may differ widely according to whether they are regarded with optimism or pessimism. Dangerous and unsound situations can be tided over if the public trusts its leaders, while even the most inherently sound situation is no safeguard against panic and collapse if confidence in them is shaken.

The favourable tone of Stock Exchanges all over the world until 1929 was largely due to the faith of financial circles, as well as of the general public, in a number of prominent financiers, most of whom rose to fame after the war. They were amazingly successful, and acquired a reputation for being infallible. Their task was comparatively easy during a period of prosperity, and their ability did not undergo a real test until the beginning of the troubles. In countries which experienced inflation after the war, the subsequent stabilisation brought about the collapse of several prominent financiers whose greatness was largely due to the conditions of fictitious prosperity created by inflation. The Stinnes fortune in Germany disappeared soon after the stabilisation of the reichsmark. In Austria, Bosel and Castiglione failed soon after the stabilisation of the krone. In other countries which did not suffer from inflation the post-war financiers had a better chance to consolidate themselves. Their rise was, perhaps, not quite as meteoric as that of Stinnes, but they had a longer period at their disposal during which to establish themselves safely. Many of them failed, however, to make use of the better opportunities.

It was the collapse of one of the most notorious post-war financiers, Clarence Hatry, that provided the occasion for the Stock Exchange slump, first in this country and soon afterwards in Wall Street. The circumstances of his failure and the magnitude of the sums involved were calculated to shake confidence, and to put financiers, banks, and the public on their guard. This failure was followed by a series of open or disguised liquidations on the part of post-war financiers. The ominous fate of the "H's" in London has become a cautionary tale in the City. Both in Great Britain and abroad there were a large number of such financial scandals calculated to undermine confidence. In London the public has generally realised how unreal and unfounded the promoting boom of 1927–1929 was, and has become distrustful towards the City. Apart from the notorious affairs such as the Hatry case, there were dozens of smaller scandals inflicting heavy losses upon disillusioned investors. In France, the Gazette du

Franc case and the Oustric affair produced a similar result; in fact, the latter brought about a wave of distrust even against the leading commercial banks, whose counterparts have always been above suspicion in London. The fact that leading politicians and active members of the Government were involved in the Oustric scandal created distrust towards the authorities themselves.

In Italy there were a series of scandals in the course of the last two years. The case of the Banca Italo-Britannica, which caused exceptionally heavy losses to the British interests which controlled that institution, was the most notorious example. Although it is a matter of general knowledge that the managements of branches and affiliated banks on the Continent do speculate sometimes with the funds and credit of the bank under their charge, the magnitude of the figures involved in the Banca Italo-Britannica affair was probably without precedent. Another scandal of equal dimensions was the liquidation of the Gualino group. To characterise the boldness of Signor Gualino's activities, it is sufficient to mention that he attempted to acquire control of the Credito Italiano, the second largest bank of Italy, and of the Crédit Lyonnais, the leading bank of France, and that he very nearly succeeded in attaining his object. He was, at one time, regarded as the ablest financier and the richest man in Europe. To-day he is confined to Lipari Island as a penalty for the damages he inflicted upon the economic life of Italy. It was his fall that caused the collapse of the Oustric group, with which he was closely associated.

Germany also had her share of financial scandals, the most outstanding being the affair of the Frankfurter Allgemeine Versicherungs-A.-G. Belgium was disillusioned even before the beginning of the crisis as a result of her losses incurred in the Loewenstein securities. In Belgium and Spain, the circumstances of the spectacular rise and subsequent liquidation of the Cork Trust of Señor Pereña tended to discourage the public. Denmark had also her Hatry affair: the collapse of the Plum group will be remembered there for some time to come. In Austria, the heavy losses of the Österreichische Creditanstalt, which had to be reconstructed with Government support, has shaken confidence in Central Europe.

In Sweden the circumstances of the collapse of the Kreuger group have dealt a severe blow upon international confidence. As Ivar Kreuger was, until the day of his suicide, regarded as an exceptional financial genius, and his integrity was above suspicion, the disappointment caused by the revelations as to his fraudulent dealings have produced a profound effect upon the mentality of bankers and investors alike.

In the United States, a scandal of the first magnitude has been that of the Bank of the United States, which failed at the end of 1930. Although the Bank of the United States, in spite of its high-sounding name, was always regarded as a third-rate institution, the amount involved in its failure was considerable. It was easily the biggest failure in the history of American banking. Owing to its circumstances, its failure inspired distrust in a number of other banks and brought about a run on banks in general. Several American banking houses, whose names are household words in the United States and also in banking communities abroad, got into difficulties and had to be reconstructed.

The fact that leading American bankers and statesmen failed to foresee the crisis—in fact, they expressed themselves with extreme optimism on the very eve of the Wall Street collapse—has also contributed to shake the confidence of the American public in the ability of those who manage its finances.

CHAPTER XI

OVERCAPITALISATION

IF a company increases its nominal capital above the real wealth which it has invested in the business, it will be forced to pay correspondingly less in dividends to its shareholders. The watering up of the capital of companies is contrary to the elementary principles of sound finance. If this is true as regards an individual company, there is no reason why it should be otherwise as regards a country, or even the world as a whole. As a result of the war and post-war conditions, the fictitious wealth of practically every country has been raised to a multiple of its pre-war figure. The counterpart of the enormous war debts was used up and destroyed during the war, and all that remained was the huge fictitious capital that clamoured for remuneration.

It is true that in many countries inflation reduced the real burden of this newly created paper wealth. In Germany and other countries, where inflation attained an advanced stage, war and pre-war debts have been wiped out almost completely. Even in countries such as France, where the depreciation of the currency was stopped before it could entirely destroy savings, the greater part of the deadweight debt has been wiped out. Moreover, a number of countries, such as Russia, have repudiated certain pre-existing internal and external debts, and others have concluded agreements with their creditors reducing their liabilities. Even if we take into account these reductions, the total gold value of the deadweight debt, public and private, is now many times larger than before the war. The remuneration of this deadweight debt requires heavy taxation, and the productive classes have to bear the major part of this burden.

Apart altogether from overcapitalisation through an increase of the deadweight debt, in some countries even productive capital has increased beyond normal proportions. This was to a great extent the result of the changes in the international redistribution of wealth caused by the war, and of the maldistribution of gold. During and after the war a great part of the wealth of the European belligerent countries found its way to the United States and to the neutral countries. This became the basis of considerable financial expansion in those countries. Although the American authorities endeavoured to preserve the surplus gold, and not to allow it to become the basis of a credit expansion, it is substantially true to say that the increase in the volume of bank deposits and other instruments of credit have more or less kept pace with the increase of the gold reserve.

Post-war experience is held to dispose of the belief that inadequate credit supply is the principal obstacle to the increase of general prosperity. In fact, notwithstanding the enormous overcapitalisation in most countries, complaints as to inadequate credit supplies have since the war been as loud as ever. In Great Britain, where the increase of the internal public debt by nearly 1000 per cent provided an immense basis for fresh credit supplies, there were still experts of great authority who asserted that inadequate credit supply was the main cause of the post-war economic depres-

sion. They overlooked the fact that credits in themselves do not create markets for products so long as the
cost of production compares unfavourably with that of
other countries. The argument that a further credit
expansion would have increased domestic demand for
goods has been proved untenable by the experience of
the United States. There we witnessed a spectacular
increase of domestic demand stimulated by a hidden
inflation of credit, and the result was the boom of
1927–1929, which was bound to lead to a collapse.

Undoubtedly undercapitalisation is a serious obstacle
to economic progress, but overcapitalisation is equally
undesirable; in fact, the latter is the greater of the two
evils, as it tends to upset the economic equilibrium,
and ends up by destroying the wealth it has created.

While this factor may not have played a very important part in bringing about the economic crisis, it
has certainly been responsible to a great extent for its
aggravation. So long as economic conditions are normal
the evils of overcapitalisation are not so apparent. The
amount required for the remuneration of the excessive fictitious wealth is collected and distributed and
eventually finds channels leading back to the productive classes of the community in the form of additional
purchasing power. As soon as confidence is undermined,
however, the existence of large amounts of fictitious
wealth renders the situation extremely vulnerable. The
value of this paper wealth depends entirely upon confidence. If, as the result of some shock such as an economic crisis, confidence is undermined, the securities
which represent this capital undergo a sharp depreciation, and become immobilised. This is what has taken
place during the present economic crisis.

CHAPTER XII

OVERSPECULATION

THE question whether the Wall Street boom was responsible for the crisis has been the subject of heated controversy, especially in the United States, where it provided another opportunity for the farming districts to renew an old feud against New York. In their eyes Wall Street speculators were solely responsible for the evil from which the world in general, and the United States in particular, was and is suffering. The country had been happy and prosperous, and would have continued to progress and prosper but for the wickedness of a comparatively small number of New York financiers, whose excessive speculative activities brought about an unreasonable rise in security prices in Wall Street. The inevitable consequence of this rise was a collapse, which again brought about the destruction of immense wealth and purchasing power, and resulted in a general depression in the United States and all over the world.

To the superficial observer the indictment appears quite convincing. After all, the Wall Street slump was the first symptom of the crisis, and the connection between it and the world-wide depression is too obvious to be ignored. It is equally manifest that, but for the speculative fever in Wall Street from the end of 1927 to October 1929, the slump would never have reached anything like the dimensions it has recently attained. It may well be asked, however, whether those who regard the Wall Street slump as the cause of the crisis do not mistake cause for effect. A favourite argument of the apologists of Wall Street is that Wall Street is not any more responsible for the crisis than a fall in the barometer can be blamed for bad weather. According to them, the Stock Exchange is merely an indicator of economic tendencies, and the slump in Wall Street was fully justified by the coming economic crisis. The fact that the slump preceded the crisis only shows that the Stock Exchange is a highly sensitive indicator of events before they actually materialise.

The truth lies somewhere between the two extremes. It would be unreasonable to put all the blame on Wall Street for the world crisis. Speculators were certainly not responsible for the agricultural and industrial overproduction which resulted in an accumulation of stocks. Nor were they responsible for the underconsumption in various countries caused by a variety of circumstances. Nor can they be blamed for the maldistribution of gold, or for the disturbed equilibrium caused by sudden changes in production and consumption. It is true that their excessive optimism before the slump and their excessive pessimism after the Wall Street break was responsible, to a great extent, for bringing about and accentuating the crisis, but they were not by any means the only people whose optimism and pessimism were exaggerated. The whole of the United States, and, to a much lesser extent, also other countries, were characterised by excessive optimism in 1928 and 1929. This optimism revealed itself not only in gambling on the Stock Exchange, but also in a too rapid increase of production and also in excessive spending on the part of consumers. All these and other factors had their due share in the responsibility for the crisis.

At the same time it cannot be denied that events in Wall Street during 1928 and 1929 were largely to blame. The comparison between Wall Street and the barometer is not very appropriate, for the barometer cannot influence the weather, while the Stock Exchange could, and did, influence the economic situation. In Chapter VIII. we pointed out that the monetary factor contributed to a great extent in bringing about the crisis. Although the maldistribution of gold was primarily responsible for this, the drain of funds to Wall Street, in the form of loans to brokers and purchases of American shares, accentuated the abnormal monetary situation. But for the Wall Street boom there would not have been any need for the increase of bank rates all over the world, and it would have been easier to deal with the French gold demand, perturbing as it was.

Moreover, it was a consequence of the Wall Street boom that the United States in 1928 practically stopped lending abroad. As a result of the boom, both the banks and the investing public lost interest in foreign loans, and sold out their holding of European bonds so as to "play the market" (as speculation in stocks was described). Thus they not only ceased to supply Europe and the other continents with fresh capital, but actually resold them a great part of the bonds issued in previous years. As will be seen in a subsequent chapter, this factor has also contributed to bringing about the crisis. Over and above all, the Wall Street boom was a main cause of the crisis by creating an immense fictitious wealth during 1928 and 1929. The exaggerated rise of stock-market prices, which was entirely unjustified by existing economic conditions—prosperous though they were—added milliards of dollars to the apparent spending power of the American public and, to a much lesser extent, also to that of the European public. The Wall Street collapse and the subsequent declines in European Stock Exchanges annihilated this fictitious wealth in the course of a few months. Overspending was followed by a strict curtailment of spending which naturally contributed towards accentuating and prolonging the crisis. There is no reason to assume that, but for the Wall Street boom, the world would have altogether escaped its present economic crisis. It is highly probable, however, that this crisis would have been much milder, and, possibly, would merely have assumed the form of more or less prolonged economic depression. It would, however, have taken place in any case, owing to the anomalies and disequilibrium which developed since the war in economic life itself, and which needed readjustment.

So far as the Wall Street boom was responsible for the difficulties, the whole burden of its share in the blame does not fall upon the shoulders of the community of bankers, brokers, and professional speculators. The public in the United States—and to a much less extent in other countries—joined professional elements in the gamble. But for their whole-hearted participation, the boom would have remained within modest limits. Admittedly those financiers and statesmen who used their authority for encouraging rather than discouraging the public in its gambling fever are largely to blame for this, but the readiness with which the public followed their advice should be borne in mind.

CHAPTER XIII

SOVIET ACTIVITIES

As it is the declared aim of the Soviet Union to destroy the capitalist system all over the world, it is only natural that the Soviet Government should be under permanent suspicion, and that any political or economic troubles, wherever they occur, should be regarded as Communist handiwork. It has become a habit to attribute every evil to Soviet activities, and in this the present crisis is by no means exceptional. There is no reason to suppose that these activities contributed to any extent to the origin of the crisis, but there is little doubt that they played a fairly important part in aggravating the depression.

Dumping of commodities by Soviet export organisations had a certain share in the fall of world prices and accentuated the crisis, especially in certain countries directly affected. This dumping is part of the much discussed Five Years Plan. In order to be able to pay for the machinery required for the building up of powerful industries, the Soviet Government has to sell its produce to the foreign markets. As it has absolute control over all economic activity in the Soviet Union, it is in a position to fix the price of its exported produce as low as is desirable from the point of view of the success of its policy. It is hardly reasonable to assume that the Soviet authorities brought about deliberately a fall of prices of their principal export articles, such as wheat, timber, and oil. After all, they stand to lose if the proceeds of their exports are reduced by the fall of prices. They did not lower prices beyond the figure at which they could successfully compete with other producing countries, for, from their point of view, price-cutting was merely a necessary evil and not an end in itself. From the point of view of the result on world prices, the motive makes, however, little difference. There can be no doubt that the fall in the price of timber and oil was largely the result of forced Soviet exports, and that Soviet wheat exports had an important influence in bringing down wheat prices in an already declining market.

Another way by which Soviet activities contributed to the fall of prices was the peculiar system of borrowing to which they resorted in the absence of adequate normal credit resources. They bought various goods on credit and resold them at once at a lower price for cash. *NB* In doing so they suffered a substantial loss, but they considered it worth their while, as it enabled them to acquire machinery which they needed for the execution of their Five Years Plan. Expensive as this method of borrowing appears, it is in fact cheaper than the rate at which Soviet authorities could borrow in the open market. In spite of the decline of money rates all over the world, the rate at which Soviet bills can be placed in London or other leading centres is still about 20 to 24 per cent per annum. On the other hand, they can easily obtain goods credits at normal rates of interest. As a result of depressed conditions, holders of commodity stocks are only too willing to sell their surplus to the Soviet on a credit basis. The interest usually charged on such transactions is about 5 or 6 per cent per annum: thus, if the Soviet authorities buy goods on a two years' credit and sell them at a loss of, say, 20 per cent, spread over a period of two years, this 20 per cent only represents 10 per cent per annum, so that the cost of the operation is merely 15 to 16 per cent per annum. This compares favourably with the rate at which the Soviet could borrow, apart altogether from the fact that the extent to which it could borrow even at 20 to 24 per cent is very restricted. Here again, as in the case of forced exports, the object of selling below current market prices was not to bring about a fall, but to provide funds for their own requirements. Nevertheless, it has had the effect of accentuating the fall to no slight extent, especially in certain commodities such as zinc, for instance, or textiles in Poland.

In some instances it has been stated, however, that the Soviet agents aim deliberately at demoralising the market. Although the newly created Soviet industries are unable to satisfy more than a small part of the requirements of the population, some experiments have already been carried out to export some of their products. These exports are not, of course, essential to the Soviet Union, as the demand for exportable goods of these kinds is limited. In order to produce the strongest possible effect upon the market, the agents in charge of selling these goods are said to have misled the market by promising to supply in future larger quantities at low prices. As a consequence, it has become difficult for legitimate sellers to find buyers for these products at prices higher than those quoted by the Soviet agents. Such operations are, however, the exception rather than the rule. They show, nevertheless, that the accentuation of the decline of prices forms part of the policy of the Soviet Government.

Immediately after the war hopes were entertained in Moscow, and not altogether unreasonably, that the disturbed economic conditions might lead to a world revolution, but gradually these hopes were abandoned during the subsequent period of gradual stabilisation and progress towards adjustment. The present world crisis has brought about a revival of these expectations. It is assumed that, should the crisis develop into a panic and a general economic collapse, the work of Soviet propaganda would become much easier. The millions of unemployed might provide excellent material for engineering a world revolution, and the crisis provides an excellent argument against the capitalist system. For this reason the fall of prices suits their political purposes, even though, economically, it may cause them losses. As their political and economic interests are, therefore, to some extent conflicting, they had to compromise, inasmuch as they did not deliberately accentuate the fall of prices except in cases where the economic interests involved were not very considerable.

It has been repeatedly stated that several deliberate attempts have been made to create panics and to engineer runs on banks. It is difficult to express any opinion as to how much truth there is in these allegations. In one instance at least, in the case of a well-known continental bank, statements to that effect have been discredited. Although it was officially stated that the conditions of that bank were quite satisfactory and that adverse rumours were merely due to Soviet intrigues, a few weeks later the Government dismissed the board of directors of that bank, confirming by its action the rumours attributed to Soviet sources. This, however, does not necessarily mean that Soviet agents had no hand in engineering the runs upon banks in the United States towards the end of 1930.

The political and economic uncertainty caused by the existence of a hostile power of great importance has also contributed to delay recovery. Although it seems to be highly improbable that the Soviet will either attack or be attacked by any other power, there are, nevertheless, periodical scares which tend to perturb public opinion and the business world. Should the Five Years Plan succeed, the power of the Soviet authorities to carry on dumping will increase to no slight extent, a consideration which is calculated to make men pessimistic about the prospects of industries in other countries.

It would be a mistake, however, to attach exaggerated importance to the rôle of the Soviet in bringing about the present crisis. Overstatement can only weaken the case against them; moreover, it provides them with gratuitous advertisement.

CHAPTER XIV

THE FINANCIAL CRISIS

HITHERTO we have been discussing theories that try to explain the causes of the *economic* crisis of 1929–1931. In the present chapter we shall examine the explanations given for the *financial* crisis experienced by the world during the second half of 1931. There is, of course, no rigid line between the two periods. Although the financial crisis may be said to have originated with the difficulties of the Creditanstalt in May 1931, we have seen in Chapter II. that already towards the end of 1930 several countries, such as the United States and France, experienced severe banking crises. Moreover, the economic crisis continued unabated during the second half of 1931, and the financial crisis had grave repercussions upon the economic situation. It is nevertheless convenient to treat the economic crisis and the financial crisis as two distinct periods. Until the summer of 1931 it appeared as if the economic crisis would take its normal course, as described in economic textbooks. It did not essentially differ from any of the prewar crises; in fact, in many ways it was milder than some of the crises experienced in the past. Developments during the second half of 1931 have, however, made us realise that we are confronted by an entirely abnormal situation, which is not subject to the influence of factors which usually operate in crises. At the same time we had to realise that a number of abnormal factors were at work as a result of which the economic depression developed into a financial crisis of unprecedented dimensions threatening the very foundations of capitalism and civilisation.

Towards the middle of 1931 many people began to realise that the difference between the present crisis and past crises is not merely one of degree. In the past the low interest rates brought about by the crisis resulted in a tendency towards the revival of trade. On the present occasion, however, the prolonged cheapness of money all over the world has failed to produce the least effect. It did not create additional demand for credit, nor did it drive idle funds into business. Although both commodities and securities have declined to levels at which they were described by market experts as being "within buying range", the decline failed to stimulate buying. Although in theory the fall of world prices tended to remedy the evil of inadequate gold supplies, in practice the shortage of gold was as acute when the prices have declined below pre-war levels as it was when the index numbers were in the vicinity of 140.

The reason why low interest rates and low prices failed to produce their normal effect was that the world anticipated further declines, and a prolonged state of depression. In such circumstances the spirit of enterprise was naturally at a low ebb. Political uncertainty was mainly responsible for the general feeling of pessimism. It was widely anticipated that the reparations controversy would come to a climax in the near future. The proposal of the Austro-German Customs Union scheme created an atmosphere of tension in international politics, and resulted in a set-back after a moderate recovery early in 1931. Before very long the political factor was to assume predominant importance, and was mainly responsible for the development of the financial crisis.

While the total gold supply available for monetary purposes may have been inadequate to cover requirements when prices were about 40 per cent above their pre-war level, the shortage of gold ought to have become a progressively less important force as prices first approached and then fell below the levels of 1913. Unfortunately the world did not benefit by the decline of prices, for throughout 1930 and 1931 the maldistribution of gold had become accentuated. Although the decline of world prices reduced normal requirements, the amounts thus released found their way to France and the United States, Holland and Switzerland, where they have become sterilised. As a result, towards the middle of 1931 the shortage of gold was as acute as two years earlier. It is thus no wonder that the trend of world prices continued to point downward. The prolonged economic crisis and political tension have undermined confidence, and the Creditanstalt affair provided the last straw. Owing to the political circumstances surrounding the difficulties of this bank, it has become the starting-point of a violent wave of distrust which at first confined itself to Central Europe, but which spread rapidly all over the world.

The following are the principal theories aiming at explaining the financial crisis of 1931:

(1) Excessive borrowing by Germany.

(2) Failure of the gold standard.

(3) The introduction of politics into the sphere of international finance.

There is no doubt about it that through borrowing on

an excessive scale Germany and her creditors have rendered themselves vulnerable. As a result of the increase of Germany's external short-term indebtedness, the German currency and banking system was exposed to a collapse if anything interfered with the inflow of funds. By lending to Germany on an excessive scale foreign centres exposed themselves to severe shocks through any difficulties in Germany. It is beyond doubt that so long as the problem of Reparations remained unsettled, the implicit confidence in Germany's solvency shown by bankers was unjustified.

At the same time, bankers could not be expected to foresee the full gravity of the situation which has arisen towards the middle of 1931 as the result of the coincidence of a number of most unusual circumstances. The excessive borrowing by Germany abroad was a not unnatural consequence of the fixing of Reparations at a figure that was above Germany's capacity to pay. Thus, so far as excessive German borrowing was responsible for the crisis, Germany and foreign banks who lent to her are less to blame than the Governments which fixed Reparations at an unduly high figure.

It has become a commonplace of newspaper articles that the accentuation of the economic depression into a financial crisis has been due to the failure of the gold standard to fulfil its functions in the changed circumstances. There is no doubt about it that, as we explained in Chapter VIII., the changed post-war situation resulted in an abnormally heavy strain upon the gold standard. In spite of this the system could have continued to function amidst all the difficulties caused by the economic crisis but for the banking crisis that arose independently of any deficiency of the gold standard. For it is well to remember that the wave of distrust

against the stability of foreign exchanges was merely
the consequence of distrust in banks. In Austria the
Creditanstalt crisis did not affect the stability of the
exchange, and in Germany the fears of a collapse of the
reichsmark were merely the result of the heavy withdrawals of foreign funds brought about by the distrust
of foreign creditors against German banks. In London,
too, unjustified fears as to the repercussions of the
German crisis upon the banking situation were largely
responsible in the beginning for the flight from the
pound. It was only at a later stage that the banking
crisis developed into a currency crisis.

The political factor has played an important part in
accentuating the crisis. Suspicion of banks and currencies was largely due to uncertainty in the sphere of
international politics, and to the introduction of politics
into the sphere of international finance. The part
played by this factor is described in detail in the
author's books *Behind the Scenes of International
Finance* (Macmillan, 1931) and *Finance and Politics*
(Macmillan, 1932). Here we shall confine ourselves to
pointing out that, but for inadequate international
co-operation, the calamity of 1931 would never have
occurred. French reparations policy was responsible for
the development of the highly dangerous situation of
German short-term indebtedness; the endeavours of
France to accumulate a large gold stock for political
purposes have largely contributed to weaken London's
resisting capacity; the open clash between French and
British interests over the Creditanstalt affair, and the
delay in the acceptance by France of the Hoover
Moratorium have been largely responsible for the alarm
which precipitated the financial crisis. There is no
doubt that the postponement of the Lausanne Con-

ference from January to June was largely responsible for the prolongation of the crisis. The French attitude in regard to the credits granted to the Reichsbank by a group of central banks, and in regard to the Danubian Scheme, has accentuated the uneasiness as to the possible influence of the political factor.

PART III
THE WAY OUT

CHAPTER XV

HOPEFUL SIGNS

UNDER the influence of the crisis, the public is inclined to regard the future with exaggerated pessimism. During the boom the view was widely held that the war had fundamentally changed our economic system, so that prosperity need not be followed by relapse, and could go on increasing for ever. Since the slump public sentiment has been reversed, and now it is widely believed that, while before the war every period of depression ended sooner or later in a revival, the present crisis constitutes a turning-point in the economic history of western civilisation, and the decline which began at the end of 1929 will go on for ever, and will result in a complete collapse of civilisation, the establishment of Soviet Republics all over the world, or at least a permanent reduction in the standard of living. Needless to say, both assumptions are equally unreasonable and highly harmful. The belief in everlasting and uninterrupted prosperity was mainly responsible for the reckless gambling fever in Wall Street, and had also a share in the responsibility for overproduction and overspending. The present pessimistic view of an everlasting depression is unquestionably responsible for the accentuation and prolongation of the crisis. Many people believe that, if only optimism could be revived,

85

normal conditions could soon be restored. Even if this view cannot be accepted at its face value, there is a great deal to be said for it. It is, therefore, important that the public should be able to see the crisis in its true significance without exaggeration, and that it should realise that, although conditions are grave, they are by no means desperate.

It ought to be borne in mind that the resisting capacity of the world is incomparably greater than it was during previous crises. Although the dimensions of the present calamity are much larger than those of any previous crisis, the sufferings inflicted upon mankind are less severe. In spite of the extreme poverty of many individuals, people are not allowed to starve in any part of the civilised world. The victims of the crisis are given a certain minimum assistance, whether in the form of support by the authorities or through the activities of charitable organisations. In this respect the situation compares favourably even with the post-war crisis in Central Europe.

The destruction of wealth caused by the present crisis, formidable as it is, is almost entirely fictitious. The reduction of savings as the result of unemployment, and the depreciation of securities, cannot be regarded in the same light as the material destruction caused by the war in France or by the earthquake in Japan. To some extent the plant of industrial enterprise deteriorates through disuse, but, generally speaking, the material wealth created since the war does not disappear as a result of the crisis. Nor is the depreciation of the fictitious wealth comparable with the wholesale destruction of fictitious wealth caused by post-war inflation. Even in Germany, with its unemployment of over four millions, the average citizen is not suffering physically to the same extent as he was in 1923, when industries enjoyed an apparent prosperity through inflation.

It would be idle to attempt to minimise the gravity of the situation. There is no doubt that we are experiencing the worst economic crisis of modern history. Although some of the crises before the war were perhaps more violent, the world got over them in a comparatively short time. On no previous occasion has the crisis spread over practically the whole world, and affected practically every section of economic life. The losses inflicted by the present crisis are far greater than those caused by any previous crisis, even if we allow for the general increase of wealth during the last few decades. The crisis has now been going on for nearly three years, and there is no indication to justify any optimism as to its early termination. Notwithstanding all this, the outlook is by no means hopeless.

One of the favourable consequences of the crisis is the establishment of closer co-operation between rival banks. Bankers realise that during periods of depression cut-throat competition is out of place, and that it is not in the interests of any bank that its rival should fail, because a big failure may easily create a general panic, which may threaten the existence of every bank. It is a hopeful sign that the obvious truth of this fact has been duly admitted, and that in most cases where a bank of standing has got into a difficult position support has been forthcoming from other banking interests. In cases where this support was not sufficient, the authorities themselves have stepped in to help the bank in difficulties. It has been realised that the Government of a country cannot be indifferent to the fate of its leading banking houses. While Governments do not, as a rule, step in to save commercial or industrial firms, however large, the position is different as regards banks. The failure of a bank affects many thousands of people, and it is, therefore, both politically and economically desirable for a Government to prevent it. From the point of view of the external credit of a country, the failure of a leading bank is much more damaging than that of any other type of business enterprise. For these reasons, the authorities in several countries have been prepared to stand considerable losses so as to prevent the failure of big banks. In some cases there was no direct Government assistance, but the authorities brought pressure to bear upon leading banks to co-operate in reconstruction. Unfortunately, in several instances in continental countries, the assistance came too late and did not prevent the failure of the banks, but helped in their reconstruction or at least indemnified certain special classes of creditors, such as small depositors or foreign creditors. As the official quarters had to sacrifice considerable amounts in the end, it would have been wiser to lend their aid in good time so as to prevent failure with all its bad moral effects.

Another factor which has tended to mitigate the crisis, at least in its earlier stages, has been international co-operation. In this respect conditions have changed for the worse since the accentuation of the crisis. But, if we compare the present state of affairs with pre-war conditions, it is impossible not to recognise the immense progress that has been made. In the first place, there is the League of Nations, which has rendered useful services since the war in assisting particular countries to overcome their economic and financial difficulties. The movement of co-operation of central banks has also rendered very useful services to the same end. Before the war it was simply unthinkable that central banks should consult each other before making changes in their bank rates, and that they should be induced to adjust their monetary policy to some extent to the requirements of other markets. It has now been realised that money markets are interdependent, and difficulties in one market cannot fail to affect the position of the other markets. For this reason it is to the interest of every central bank to assist in maintaining stability, not only in its own respective markets, but also in the rest of the world. The Bank for International Settlements was established largely for this end. Although the Bank has not been in existence for a sufficiently long period to develop all its possibilities, it has already rendered some useful services during the crisis.

As the effects of the crisis grew more serious, every Government felt itself compelled to take active steps to protect its own interests. It is regrettable that the actions they took were so often damaging to the interests of their neighbours and that so little co-operation took place. In face of the danger of a collapse, the authorities and banking interest of most countries have adopted the selfish and short-sighted policy of trying to save themselves irrespective of other interests, and, if necessary, at the expense of other interests. This mentality has largely contributed to the aggravation of the crisis. Unless this is a temporary phase, and unless the necessity for co-operation is realised in every country, the prospects before western civilisation are dark indeed.

CHAPTER XVI

RESTORATION OF CONFIDENCE

THERE can be little doubt that the crisis is due more to psychological than material causes. Although a number of material factors have contributed towards the world's difficulties, lack of confidence and excessive pessimism undoubtedly bear a large share of the responsibility for our troubles. Unless these disturbing factors can be eliminated, there is little hope of regaining prosperity through some improvement of the material circumstances. Thus it would be of little use to destroy by common agreement the unsaleable surplus products which are to be found in all the chief producing countries of the world, and the existence of which is undoubtedly one of the causes of the crisis, so long as there is no likelihood of a revival of optimism of the public, without which enterprising spirit will remain at a low ebb, consumption will continue to decline, and the process of deterioration will go on unabated. It is equally useless to attempt to bring about a rise in world prices by increasing the means of payment so long as a pessimistic public is not inclined to buy. The first and most important step towards recovery is to restore confidence, and to create an atmosphere of hope.

One of the principal sources of pessimism is the uncertainty of the international political outlook. The

controversy over Reparations has created a tension
which has a strong unsettling effect on the mind of
the public ; nor is the tension confined to the countries
directly concerned with Reparations. We have seen
that an improvement in the international political
situation early in 1931 resulted in a moderate economic
recovery, while the adverse turn of international relations brought about a relapse, and was responsible for
the accentuation of the crisis in the summer of 1931.
The Lausanne Agreement, reducing the amount of
Reparations to £150 millions, is conditional to a corresponding reduction of war debts. Failing that, the
question would be reopened again. So long as the
public is not reassured in this respect, there is no hope
for any economic recovery. The only way to reassure
the world is to conclude a definite agreement as to war
debts. Any temporary arrangements such as the prolongation of the moratorium for another year or two,
or the reduction of the amount of the annuities for a
certain number of years, would fail to produce a re-
assuring effect, as everybody would anticipate a renewal
of the conflict when the period of complete or partial
moratorium was over. The solution of the crisis lies with
the American Government. So long as France maintained her stubborn attitude as to Reparations, there
was no hope for the mitigation of the crisis. As the
American attitude towards war debts largely affects
the outlook for a settlement of Reparations, the United
States has now a grave responsibility in this matter. A
solution has to be found in which each party consents
to sacrifices in the interests of a return of political and
economic stability. Any delay only aggravates the
situation, and renders it more difficult to find an
acceptable solution.

In order to restore confidence it is necessary to re-establish the whole-hearted international co-operation in the economic and financial sphere that has suffered a sharp set-back as a result of the crisis. Although the Bank for International Settlements provides an excellent medium for financial co-operation, the use which has been made of it for that purpose has been and is still inconsiderable. It is true that in the present circumstances the Bank is unable to give assistance to any country as its resources are largely tied up in the advances that it has already made, but there is no reason why the Bank should not be used more extensively for co-operation in such technical matters as the establishment of a foreign exchange clearing. An attempt to overcome the difficulties caused by exchange restrictions through the intermediary of the Bank for International Settlements did not have the desired results. It would be a mistake, however, to give up the idea, for in the technical sphere the Bank could render valuable services even at a time when Governments have not reached any agreement upon fundamental principles. It is to the interest of every country to overcome the present deadlock caused by exchange restrictions, and a common basis could be used for co-operation to that end, irrespective of any controversies that may be going on for some time on vital political and economic issues. Once the problem of Reparations is settled, the restoration of confidence will pave the way towards international co-operation for the restoration of monetary stability. Although it would be perhaps unduly optimistic to expect that the principal holders of gold would consent to a pooling of their surplus with the Bank for International Settlements, some formula may eventually be found for providing a channel

for a better distribution of gold through the intermediary of the Bank.

Although the restoration of confidence is primarily
an international problem, a great deal can be done to
that end in every country independently of the international solution of the problem. The restoration of
internal political stability in every country through
the co-operation of all political parties and all classes
would go a long way towards restoring confidence, and
would also facilitate progress towards international
understanding. A country with a stable Government
backed by every section of the nation inspires confidence at home and abroad. In an economic sphere
much could be done for the restoration of confidence
through the consolidation of industrial and commercial
enterprises by means of amalgamations. The crisis has
eliminated the weaker elements in every country, but
those companies which have survived have lost much
of their strength. It would be desirable to combine
them into stronger units, especially as the reduction in
the number of units facilitates co-operation between
them.

Once confidence is restored economic recovery may
take place with an astonishing suddenness. Amidst the
crisis one is always inclined to take a gloomy view as
to the prospects of recovery. In 1923, when the European currency chaos attained its climax, few people
dared to hope that within a few years monetary
stability would be restored, and yet by 1926 practically
all currencies were stabilised, and most budgets were
balanced. The same phenomenon may repeat itself
again. Once the factors responsible for distrust are eliminated, economic conditions may improve with surprising rapidity. The world would realise that from a

material point of view nothing has been lost through
the crisis. The soil is as productive as it was in the
height of prosperity. Mineral wealth and other natural
resources, which are, after all, the foundation of prosperity, have remained unchanged. The immense assets
represented by industrial plants, railways and all other
means of communication, buildings in towns and villages,
and innumerable other forms of wealth have remained
unchanged. The skill and health of communities has not
been seriously impaired. Had all this disappeared as
a result of the crisis, there would be good reason to
despair. As it is, nothing irreparable has happened.
Once confidence is restored, economic life will resume
its normal course, even though it may take some time
before conditions become adjusted to the changes that
have taken place during the last few years.

CHAPTER XVII

NATIONAL SOLUTION

IT has been hoped that the solution of the crisis will come through international co-operation. The events of the last few months have, however, shaken these hopes. The gravity of the situation has failed to bring the nations together in closer co-operation. On the contrary, the worse conditions became, the less willing the nations of the world appeared to be prepared to consider each other's interests. Until September 1931 there appeared to be a kind of solidarity between countries on a gold basis for the mutual safeguard of each other's currencies. Since Great Britain's departure from gold this solidarity has ceased. Moreover, every country has adopted a policy of safeguarding its interests by some form of restriction of imports. Apart from the introduction of new customs duties, and the increase of the existing ones, the official regulation of the sale of foreign exchanges in many countries has also aimed at restricting the amount of goods bought abroad.

It appears that every country is now endeavouring to work out its own salvation by pursuing a Mercantilist policy. As a result of the breakdown of the endeavours to establish international co-operation this appears to be the only alternative. Undoubtedly every country stands to lose by it in certain directions. Well-established trade relations are artificially broken up, inflicting heavy losses upon exporters in every country. Moreover, the endeavour to satisfy the greater part of the requirements by national production is bound to lead to a further increase of productive capacity, although one of the causes of the present crisis is exactly excessive increase of production.

In spite of its obvious disadvantages, there is a great deal to be said in favour of the attempt to solve the crisis on national lines. Possibly it may eventually lead to the establishment of international co-operation. One of the reasons why some countries have been unwilling to co-operate whole-heartedly has been that they have considered themselves sufficiently independent to disregard the interests of others. The endeavours to solve the crisis on national lines will make these countries realise how much they stand to gain, and how much they stand to lose, by the result of their policy.

There is no doubt that the revival of economic nationalism brought about by the crisis will lead to a reduction in the standard of living in many countries. The result of the endeavours to produce the greater part of the requirements at home will be that goods will be produced in less favourable conditions. But the disadvantages of this will be compensated to a great extent by the greater stability of economic conditions in every country. One of the great disadvantages of the internationalisation of our economic system has been that prosperity in most countries has been made dependent to a too great extent upon conditions in other countries. The development of new industries abroad under the protection of customs barriers would at any time inflict heavy losses upon the exporting industries, while even agriculture and the production of raw materials have not been immune from such unfavourable changes.

The object of the present economic nationalism is to safeguard as far as possible the home market for national production. It is, of course, inevitable that a great part of the requirements should be met by imports. In this respect the tendency points towards the adoption of a system of international barter. A manufacturing country is prepared to buy agricultural products provided that the agricultural country is willing to buy an equivalent amount of manufactures. There could be, of course, no question of laying down hard and fast rules that we shall buy exactly the equivalent of the amount of goods we sell abroad, for in that case our debtors would not be in a position to repay their debts. But as a matter of principle buying each other's goods will be based on reciprocity.

It is impossible to say at this stage whether this development will be merely a temporary device adopted under the pressure of the crisis, or whether in substance it will survive the emergency. It seems probable that the movement towards a greater freedom of international trade through the establishment of Customs Unions has suffered a lasting set-back, and that it will take some time before the wave of economic nationalism spends its force. Even if the restrictions of imports are at present meant to be temporary, they are bound to lead to the development of production in every country, which will afterwards necessitate the consolidation of the progress thus attained by means of permanent customs barriers. The immediate effect of the changes will be to aggravate the crisis in many countries. In the absence of an international solution, how-

H

ever, there seems to be no alternative but to attempt to solve the crisis on national lines.

In this respect Great Britain and the British Empire are at a considerable advantage, as they form a practically self-contained unit. The Dominions and Colonies could produce all the food and raw material required by the mother-country, and provide immense possibilities for the development of potential markets for British manufactures. This does not mean that Great Britain will cut adrift economically from the rest of the world, only that she will in future base her relations with foreign countries on the rule of give and take. Provided that close co-operation can be established between the various members of the Empire, Great Britain and the Dominions and Colonies stand a better chance to work out their salvation on national lines than almost any other country.

Notwithstanding this, the policy of the British Government should be to aim at an international rather than a national solution, provided that in future other Governments show greater willingness to co-operate than they have done in the past.

CHAPTER XVIII

INFLATION OR DEFLATION?

SINCE times immemorial monetary policy has always been the favourite hunting-ground of bold reformers. Taking it for granted that money is the root of all evil, they believe that by means of skilful manipulation of monetary policy it is possible to cure every trouble this world is suffering from and to bring about the much-desired millennium. During the present crisis they have been particularly active in putting forward suggestions. There have been signs that quarters representing official monetary policy are no longer as orthodox and rigid as they were in the past, and this has raised hopes in currency reformers that their opportunity has come.

In fact, even those who have been tempted to accept the view of currency reformers have to realise, on the basis of the experience of the present crisis, the futility of their doctrines. An expansion of credit would not in the least remedy our situation, and in addition it is doubtful whether an expansion would be possible at all. Throughout the crisis—apart from an interval between June 1931 and March 1932—money has been cheaper and more plentiful at present than it has been for many decades, and, in spite of this, trade has not made full use of the funds available. Demand for credit was very slack, and the only way in which banks could have increased the volume of outstanding

credits would have been through indiscriminate lending without adequate security. Their customers of
standing who could provide security did not want
to increase their loans because of the depressed conditions of trade. It is not until trade begins to revive
that the expansion of credit will become practical.
The fallacy of the conception that money could be
"pumped" into circulation, and that it would act as a
tonic to economic life, has been amply proved by the
experience of the present crisis. According to a popular
belief, the reduction of bank rates is calculated to bring
about sooner or later a trade revival. During every
stage of the crisis many economists and bankers ad-
vocated a policy of cheap money, on the ground that
low interest rates are bound to force idle money into
business. The experience of the present crisis has
proved, however, that the effect of low interest rates
upon business is not as strong as is generally supposed.
Investors are not likely to buy ordinary shares merely
because they get a low interest on their deposits; after
all, the difference between the highest and lowest deposit rates paid by the British clearing banks since the
war is merely 4 per cent, while the possible loss of
capital through depreciation of shares is many times
more. So long as the public expects a further decline in
security prices it is prepared to leave its money in banks
even without interest rather than to run the risk of
capital depreciation. There is no reason to suppose that
a reduction of deposit rates tends to induce business
firms to use their idle funds for the purchase of commodities, so long as commodity prices have a downward trend and the demand remains slack. Nor is there
any likelihood of inducing manufacturers to increase
their production or extend their plant merely because

they pay $\frac{1}{2}$ per cent or 1 per cent less on their loans, so long as an increased demand and steadier prices do not justify an increase of their output.

Because in the past a period of cheap money was usually followed by a trade revival, many people are inclined to assume that the latter was the result of the former. As a matter of fact, cheap money usually accompanies trade depression, and, as depression has always been followed by revival, cheap money cannot help preceding revival. The extent to which it contributes to improve business conditions is much smaller than is generally supposed. Low interest rates have certainly a favourable psychological effect, and from that point of view they are helpful in the long run. Their actual material influence is, however, negligible, and it would be unduly optimistic to attach exaggerated hopes to the effect of the all-round reduction of bank rates.

There is no reason to believe that under the present system there would be any difficulty in financing a trade revival. The public possess large balances available for reinvestment. Doubtless, if there were a sudden and spectacular trade revival it might cause some temporary inconvenience. Large funds which are at present held on deposit with banks would be withdrawn to be reinvested in industrial securities. The increased demand for loans would, therefore, coincide with a contraction of bank resources available for that purpose. There is, however, no likelihood of a sudden revival. The recovery is bound to be a slow and gradual process, and it is highly probable that the financing of this revival will not present any particularly difficult problems.

There is a distinct tendency for public opinion to

favour inflationist measures as being the best way out
of the present deadlock. This is only natural, for everybody realises by now that deflation caused by the maldistribution of gold has been the main source of our
troubles. It is thus no wonder that those who preach
inflation find an enthusiastic audience. Even people
who, in the past, were opposed to the idea of inflation
are now inclined to consider it a lesser evil than deflation; although they realise that inflation has to be
liquidated sooner or later, and that this liquidation is a
painful process, they consider it worth while to put up
with these disadvantages for the sake of breaking the
present spell of depression. They admit that inflation
would only have the effect of a dope, which might temporarily restore the vitality of the patient, but which is
inevitably followed by a relapse once the artificial
stimulus has spent its force. In spite of this they are
in favour of administering the dope in the hope that
the breathing space provided by its effect may enable
the world to find some solution of the fundamental
troubles, in which case it will be able to stand the
strain caused by the liquidation of inflation a few years
hence. They hold the view that the risk involved in the
inflationist experiment is not too great; for since the
situation could scarcely be worse than it is at present,
any change must be for the better. In their opinion, so
long as inflation is kept within moderate limits, its
damaging effect cannot be serious.

However convincing this line of argument may appear, there is an important flaw in it. We have seen
above that in the present circumstances monetary
policy could have but little effect upon trade so long as
the present wave of pessimism prevails. There is no
way of pumping funds artificially into economic life.

Unless and until there are some signs of trade revival, an extension of credit through normal channels is impossible. We have seen that in France and the United States the spectacular increase of the note circulation did not assume the characteristic symptoms of an inflation, for the simple reason that the newly issued notes were promptly hoarded by the public, and were not used for an increased spending, without which there can be no inflation in the real sense of the term.

It is often argued that Governments are in a position to inflate by carrying out ambitious schemes of public works. Undoubtedly during the earlier stages of the crisis such measures might have produced the desired effect. At present, however, they could hardly be adopted on any large scale. Practically every Government has a huge budgetary deficit, which makes it difficult, if not impossible, to raise loans for meeting the extraordinary expenditure of such public works. Any attempt to borrow for such purposes would inevitably lead to a further accentuation of distrust, which must be avoided at all costs.

At the present stage of the crisis the powers of monetary policy are destructive rather than constructive. While there is little chance of bringing about a trade revival through the deliberate policy of inflation, a policy of deflation could check any natural trend towards a revival. It would be a fatal mistake to allow orthodox monetary doctrine to stand in the way of improved economic conditions. If there is an upward trend in prices, and increasing demands for currency and credit, it should not be checked by a dogmatic application of the principles of sound currency. We have passed the stage when we can afford to sacrifice an expansion of trade for the sake of these principles, yet unfortunately they are still regarded as sacrosanct by the monetary authorities of most countries. Although orthodox deflationism is discredited in the eyes of the public, it is rooted deeply in the mentality of those responsible for official monetary policy. The declared aim of the French authorities is to continue deflation, and to convince all countries on a gold basis to pursue the same policy. A similar deflationist mentality seems to prevail in British official circles, which are determined to oppose, by restrictions of currency and credit, the beneficial effect that the depreciation of sterling upon the price level, if allowed to take its normal course, would decidedly have upon trade. The efforts to resist this natural trend are calculated to produce the same effect as a deliberate policy of deflation, and, if carried too far, they may effectively prevent a revival.

The world is in desperate need of an improvement of economic conditions, and it would be unpardonable to jeopardise the chances of such improvement out of any undue tenderness towards monetary dogmas. Our salvation lies in rising prices. Apart from its direct effect upon trade, a rising level of prices has the additional advantage of reducing the real value of the excessive fictitious wealth, a step which is a necessary preliminary to any substantial and lasting revival.

CHAPTER XIX

THE SILVER PROBLEM

WE have seen in previous chapters that the fall in the price of silver has played an important part in bringing about the crisis. It is to be feared that this factor, far from declining in importance, will have an even more depressing influence in the future. As practically every country, with the exception of China, has abandoned, or is about to abandon, silver currency, the fall of the price of this metal is likely to continue. Even China has decided in principle that the establishment of the gold standard is desirable, and intends to take steps to that end at the earliest possible moment. The danger of such a change is not imminent, for financial conditions in general and conditions in China in particular make it at present impossible to raise the large gold loan which must be a necessary preliminary to the establishment of a gold standard. At the same time the threat of a possible change is always there, and its unsettling influence upon the price of silver is continuous. Whatever the official currency may be, the population of eastern countries still possesses large amounts of silver in the form of coins, jewelry, and hoards, and a further fall in the price of silver is bound to reduce still further their savings and their purchasing power.

As an improvement in eastern markets is one of the

conditions of the return to prosperity in the manufacturing countries, it is essential that steps should be
taken to avoid a further fall in the price of silver and, if
possible, to bring about a revalorisation of that metal.
Several schemes have been put forward aiming at
establishing a system of bimetallism so as to avoid a
further depreciation of silver, or granting China a large
silver loan on condition that she retain her silver currency. We do not propose to go into the details of these
schemes, but it is necessary to point out that a return
to bimetallism is considered by most experts as highly
undesirable. In the past, the system did not work satis-
factorily, and there is no reason to believe that it would
give better service in the future. The strongest argument in favour of it is the shortage of gold. As, however,
the fall of prices to their pre-war level has gone far to
remedy this evil, there is no need to resort to the bi-
metallic system from that point of view. Desirable as it
is to raise the value of silver, most Governments would
not consider it worth their while to reorganise their
monetary system for that purpose alone. As for the pro-
posed silver loan to China, it is doubtful whether that
country would agree to abandon its right to change
its currency for the sake of such a loan, and, in any
case, it is to be feared that the operation would lead
to inflation in China and a further depreciation of silver.
After all, the proposal amounts to the putting into
circulation of huge stocks of silver hoarded at present
by the United States Government, the British Government, the Government of Indo-China, and other interested parties. As silver would circulate in China only,
it would not increase the capacity of the Chinese
market to absorb European commodities.

At the same time it is obvious that international

co-operation is essential to check the fall in the value of silver. In the first place, it is essential to induce the Chinese Government to abandon its ill-advised plan of establishing the gold standard. In any case, the scheme is likely to remain a mere proposal for many years, perhaps several decades. As the country is, politically, not consolidated, and a number of its external loans are in default, it has no chance of raising a large external loan for some years to come. Moreover, it is highly improbable that any of the big lending countries would be prepared to grant her a huge loan to enable China to abandon the silver standard; in the American market such an operation would meet with violent opposition from the silver-producing interests, and the United States Government, being itself a large holder of silver, would hardly favour such an operation. Although similar conditions do not exist to the same extent in the British, French, and Japanese loan markets, at the same time none of the authorities concerned would like to give to China the power to draw heavily upon the world's gold supplies. Considering the size of the population of the country, an immense amount of gold would be necessary to satisfy its requirements, and although the fall in the world price level has restored the equilibrium between the world's gold supplies and monetary requirements, such an exceptional demand would probably bring about a further fall in the world price level. At the same time the population of a great part of the British Dominions and Colonies, as well as of the French Colonies, possesses large amounts of silver, and the British and French Governments are not likely to view with favour any operation which would lead to the infliction of further hardships on their own colonial populations.

These factors are so evident that it is astonishing that the Chinese authorities and their American advisers have failed to realise them. In the circumstances nothing could have been worse than the course chosen of announcing their intention of abandoning silver, as it is obvious that the intention cannot be carried out for a long time to come. The only effect it produced was further to accentuate the fall in the price of silver. If it was meant to be a threat or a gesture of defiance addressed to the Western countries, it failed to fulfil its object, and the Chinese population was the principal victim of the fall in the price of the metal. In order to check a further fall and to bring about a certain extent of recovery, it is most desirable that the Chinese Government should make a declaration that it will not abandon silver for a certain period, say for another ten or fifteen years. As, in any case, it would be unable to establish the gold standard within a shorter period, the undertaking would not constitute any serious sacrifice on the part of the Chinese Government. It should be made in the form of a binding international contract, perhaps in connection with the granting of a much-needed grain credit to relieve food shortage in China. At the same time the principal holders of silver would have to undertake not to take advantage of the situation by unloading their stocks. Possibly the result would be that the Governments of other silver-using countries, which recently have decided to abandon silver, may change their minds.

While a return to bimetallism is unlikely, the chances are that the movement for the remonetisation of silver will not be altogether unsuccessful. Possibly silver may be adopted for subsidiary coinage if an agreement to that effect could be reached between the leading countries.

CHAPTER XX

As we pointed out in Chapter XIII., Soviet dumping was also an important factor which contributed to bring about and accentuate the present crisis. Whether this factor will grow more or less important depends on the success of the Five Years Plan. According to statements by Soviet authorities, the execution of the plan is making such good progress that it is likely to be completed by the end of 1932, that is to say, in four years instead of five. Even if the source of this information is prejudiced, there is no doubt that the competitive capacity of various branches of production in Soviet Russia is rapidly increasing and is likely to be much more dangerous in a few years' time than it is at present. A second Five Years Plan is now being elaborated to cover the period from 1933 to 1937, and, even if the object of the first plan is not fully attained by the end of 1932, it may be attained in the course of the second period. This means that the Soviet Union will be largely self-sufficient in a number of products which it has to import up to now, and will be in a position to throw on the world market large quantities of raw materials and cheap manufactured goods.

Nobody contests the right of a great country to endeavour to become self-sufficient and to establish markets abroad for its products. If, however, the

country resorts to unfair competition, whether for
political or for economic ends, its ambition loses
its excuse; it becomes a disturbing influence in the
world economic system tending to delay the restoration of normal conditions. It is, therefore, to the
interest of countries affected by Soviet dumping to
organise themselves into a defensive alliance. This
does not necessarily mean that a world-wide boycott of
Soviet goods should be organised; such drastic measures
should be avoided if possible. It is, however, essential
to establish a united front against any attempt to
disturb the world markets by unfair competition. The
importance of this is not sufficiently realised, either by
the authorities or by public opinion. During the past
fourteen years anti-Soviet propaganda has cried
"wolf" too often and has fallen into discredit. The
public has become accustomed to a new war-cry every
few months, and does not realise that Soviet dumping
is not a mere anti-Bolshevik slogan, but a very real
source of danger.

Being in control of both production and export
trade, the Soviet Government is in a position to organise dumping on a larger scale than has ever been
attempted in history. It is in a position to run any
one branch of industry at a heavy loss for a long
period, so as to be able to undersell its rivals abroad.
It is also in a position to increase production and reduce
domestic consumption of one particular commodity
or group of commodities to a very great extent, so
as to flood foreign markets at prices which rule out
the possibility of competition by any private enterprise for any length of time. Doubtless it has occurred
in the past, both before and after the war, that a
Government anxious to stimulate the progress of any

national branch of industry, granted that industry a subsidy—either directly or in the shape of reductions in railway tariffs, exemption from taxation, etc.—in order to enable it to sell its products abroad below cost of production. There is, however, a considerable difference between the extent to which the system can be practised in the case of a country where industry and trade are carried on by private enterprise, and in the case of Soviet Russia, where they form a State monopoly.

Hitherto Soviet dumping has been confined to foodstuffs and raw materials, such as wheat, timber, and oil. Apart from the occasional dumping of matches, textiles, and a few other articles, mainly in the Baltic countries, Persia, and China, there has not been any dumping of manufactures on a large scale. It is highly probable, however, that in a few years the Soviet authorities will be well in a position to flood the world market with a variety of manufactures. They can afford to run certain branches of trade at a loss for many years, as they would meanwhile get compensation from other branches of trade, or would meet the deficit by borrowing—or by inflation. Thus, once they have increased their productive capacity, in textiles, for instance, to a sufficient extent, they can undersell our textile industries in articles of inferior quality all over the world. They can continue to sell at abnormally low prices during a sufficiently long period to ruin their competitors. Once this is accomplished they can concentrate upon another branch of production and achieve the same end by the same methods.

Several countries have taken steps to defend themselves against Soviet dumping: in Belgium and Germany, for instance, the import of Soviet matches is prohibited; France has introduced the system of licences for the import of Soviet products. Nothing has been done so far, however, in Great Britain to protect the market against Soviet dumping. It is true that, taking a short view, this dumping has appeared more beneficial than otherwise up to the present, for it confined itself mostly to goods which this country would, in any case, have to buy abroad, and, as a result of Soviet dumping, it has been in a position to buy them cheaper. Once, however, the productive capacity of Soviet industries has increased sufficiently to enable the Soviet Government to carry on the dumping of manufactures on a large scale, they will direct their chief attack against the British domestic market for manufactures, and will undersell British textile products in Lancashire itself. Whatever views one holds about Free Trade and Protection, it is obviously necessary to take defensive measures against such attacks. As the legislative apparatus is very slow, there is not much time to lose if we want to safeguard our vital industries from a heavy blow directed against them in the home market.

As the domestic market itself cannot absorb the products of British industries, it would be highly desirable to organise the defence against Soviet dumping on an international scale so as to safeguard our external markets. The common interests involved would make an international agreement possible. Every country stands to lose heavily through Soviet dumping sooner or later. To-day it may be the turn of agricultural countries, to-morrow it will be the turn of manufacturing countries. An international agreement would certainly produce an immediate favourable effect, as it would largely contribute towards eliminating the uncertainty of trade prospects brought about by the threat of increased Soviet dumping. It would make the Soviet authorities realise that they would stand to lose by their destructive policy, and that it is to their interest to work by more peaceful economic methods. The termination of the economic warfare between the Soviet Union and the rest of the world would provide great assistance towards the restoration of prosperity.

PART IV
FUTURE PROSPECTS

CHAPTER XXI

HOW TO AVERT CRISES

ALTHOUGH the problem which requires immediate attention is how to recover from our present crisis, it is perhaps useful to think ahead and to examine the methods to be applied after our recovery in order to prevent the recurrence of our present troubles. The experience of the present crisis may prove to be very useful, and the lesson, for which we are paying such an enormously heavy price, may assist us in our endeavour to avoid in the future the mistakes of the past.

We have seen in Chapter IV. that a considerable number of experts are inclined to take a fatalistic view of the origin of the present crisis, which they consider inevitable. Their camp is divided into two sections: some of them believe that the present crisis could not be avoided because it was necessary for prices to return to their pre-war level; according to others, the crisis was an inevitable part of the trade cycle which has been going on ever since the existence of the modern economic system. Those who hold the first view are satisfied that, once prices, wages, costs of living, etc., are down to their pre-war level, there is no reason why the present crisis should recur, unless new disturbing factors appear on the scene. Those, on the other hand, who maintain that the crisis of 1929–

1931 was merely the regular periodic crisis are of opinion that the crisis will recur over and over again at intervals of seven to ten years. Although the views of the two schools of economic fatalists are diametrically opposed, there is one point in respect of which they agree: that is that there is nothing to be done to avert a crisis in future. Those who believe that the return to the pre-war level means an end of all their troubles, consider it superfluous to take any defensive measures. Those, on the other hand, who regard the recurrence of the crisis as inevitable, consider it equally superfluous to make any efforts to avoid a disaster which, in their eyes, is bound to recur no matter what we do.

The fallacy of both arguments is equally obvious. It is absurd to imagine that once the world has returned to the pre-war level it will take a long rest, and nothing exceptional or abnormal will ever happen again. We have no right to assume that the fall of prices necessarily stops at the magic figure represented by the pre-war level, and it is equally easy to imagine causes which would bring about a rise in prices to be followed by another severe relapse. Even if we were to take it for granted that the return of prices to their pre-war level restored an ideal state of affairs, we should nevertheless consider it necessary to take defensive measures against any new disturbing factor.

As for the argument that the recurrence of the crisis from time to time is inevitable, it is based on the commonplace assumption that it is impossible to change human nature. As is well known, periodic crises are mainly due to exaggerated optimism, which leads to excesses in some direction of economic activity, and which provokes a reaction in the form of

excessive pessimism. Unfortunately it is in accordance
with human nature to take it for granted that the
existing state of affairs, whether good or bad, will last
for ever, but it is a mistake to lay down the rule that
this factor cannot be modified. To a great and increasing extent optimism and pessimism can be moderated
by those whose opinion carries weight with the public.
During a period of speculative boom timely warnings
given by the Press, the Central Bank, and leading experts would tend to keep optimism within reasonable
bounds. It is somewhat more difficult to counteract
pessimism once it settles in the mind of the public, but
it is possible to do a great deal also in this respect. If,
during the Wall Street boom of 1928–1929, the leading
American authorities on finance had combined in their
efforts to warn the public that the speculation was
overdone, instead of stimulating speculation by optimistic statements, the slump would not have assumed
anything like its present proportions.

Admittedly it is impossible to hope that the feelings
of the public can be regulated at will, and so long as
our present economic system remains in operation there
will always be tendencies towards speculative booms
caused by excessive optimism, and they will always be
followed by reactions accentuated by excessive pessimism. By co-operation between those who can exert
influence over public opinion it is possible, however,
to reduce the proportions of these fluctuations. It is
equally possible to take measures to counteract the
tendencies provoked by the unreasonable attitude of
the public, and to reduce to a minimum their adverse
effect upon economic life.

We have seen that, amongst the reasons which were
responsible for the crisis, want of adequate co-opera-

tion, in the broadest sense of the term, played a prominent part. It follows that, if we want to avoid the recurrence of the crisis, the most effective means to that end is co-operation between all sections of economic forces all over the world. This co-operation should take the following forms:

(1) Closer co-operation of the authorities with producers.

(2) Closer co-operation between producers of a single product or a group of products.

(3) Closer co-operation between producers of different branches of production.

(4) Closer co-operation between producers in different countries.

(5) Closer co-operation between the authorities in different countries.

(6) Closer co-operation between employers and employees.

(7) Closer co-operation between producers, middlemen, and consumers.

(8) Closer co-operation between banks within every country.

(9) Closer co-operation between banks and monetary authorities within every country.

(10) Closer co-operation between banks in different countries.

The rôle of the authorities is particularly important, as they are in a position to induce various conflicting interests to co-operate. If necessary, they should go beyond peaceful persuasion to that end, and should make full use of their powers to bring about co-operation. The supreme end for which everybody should co-operate is to avoid in future, as far as possible, over-

production, underconsumption, and other abnormal
tendencies which threaten the equilibrium of economic
life. The public interest involved more than outweighs
the objections to Government interference with economic developments.

CHAPTER XXII

THE CASE FOR CO-OPERATION

IT is highly important that producers should co-operate with the object of avoiding overproduction, not only within the boundaries of one country, but all over the world. To some extent this is already carried out in certain branches of production. These cases are, however, exceptional, and, generally speaking, producers are entirely in the dark as to whether or not their products can possibly be absorbed by any market. It is, of course, difficult to imagine in our present economic system a complete regulation of production according to the requirements of consumers. These requirements are subject to frequent changes, and cannot be ascertained in advance even with approximate accuracy. It is possible, however, by means of co-operation and organisation, to eliminate obvious cases of overproduction. If the world's consumption of a certain commodity in a given year was, say, 100,000 tons, not even the best organisation is in the position to foretell whether next year's demand will be 80,000 or 120,000 tons. But it is possible, by means of co-operation, to prevent four or five rival countries or rival groups from producing 100,000 tons each in the hope of being able to capture the whole market for their products. It is especially this type of overproduction which is dangerous from the point of view of

122

economic equilibrium. After all, if one year's output exceeds by 20 to 30 per cent the actual demand, it does not, in itself, ruin the industry concerned, and the discrepancy can be corrected next year. It is possible, by means of co-operation, to see that a multiple of the maximum demand imaginable is not produced.

It is by no means an easy task to bring about satisfactory co-operation between the conflicting interests in the same branch of production, even within a country, much less between several countries. In fixing the quota for every producer or group of producers a great variety of considerations have to be borne in mind, and supreme diplomatic skill is required to reconcile the interests involved. As such agreements have been reached in the past in several branches of production, it proves that they are not impossible.

It is equally important to bring about co-operation between different branches of production, especially between producers of raw materials and manufacturers using those raw materials.

A closer co-operation between consumers and producers, so as to enable the former to benefit by any fall in the cost of production and to enable the latter to have a better idea of the extent of the absorbing capacity of their market, is equally desirable. This co-operation should embrace whenever possible the wholesale and retail traders, who fulfil a useful task in economic life, and whose profits are justified so long as they are kept within reasonable limits. If, however, the middle-men prevent consumers from profiting by any improvement in methods of production, as is unfortunately very often the case to-day, means should be found for their elimination, and direct contact should be established between producers and consumers.

As we pointed out before, it is highly important that the authorities should co-operate with private interests in order to avoid the repetition of the crisis. It would be desirable for every country to elaborate a kind of "Five Years Plan", and, by means of co-operation between producers of various countries under the auspices of their Governments, these "Five Years Plans" should be co-ordinated within the limit of possibility. In our present economic system it is, of course, impossible to attain perfection in this respect; for it would necessitate the complete elimination of individual initiative, which is neither possible nor desirable. A great deal can be done, however, to improve the present state of affairs.

As the distribution of credit has great influence over the trend of production, co-operation between producers could not be complete without the collaboration of banking interests. There should be closer co-operation between the banks themselves on the one hand, and between banks and central banking authorities on the other. A speculative boom can be nipped in the bud by timely credit restriction, but it is difficult, as a rule, to induce banks to cut credits when everything seems prosperous. In order to avoid crises banks should exercise self-restraint and should act sometimes in a way which, on the surface, may appear against their own interests as well as those of their customers. As no bank is likely to be willing to adopt such a policy unless its rivals act in the same way, it is essential that they should co-operate under the guidance of the authorities.

CHAPTER XXIII

CONCLUSION

WHO is to blame? That is a question which has been the centre of heated controversy ever since the beginning of the crisis. We have already seen that over-speculation on the New York Stock Exchange played a prominent part in bringing the crisis to a head. It would be, however, one-sided and exaggerated to put all the blame on the shoulders of those who encouraged speculation and of those who took part in it. The attacks directed against international finance or banking, as the principal cause of the trouble, have no justification. It is true that banks financed to some extent the Wall Street boom by yielding to the temptation of high rates of interest paid on call money in New York. The major portion, however, of the funds financing the boom, whether through brokers' loans or direct share purchases, came from the American public itself. Everybody in the United States, big or small, speculated on a large scale. The responsibility for the Wall Street slump is shared, therefore, by millions of people. Those who were short-sighted enough to encourage speculation have, of course, a large share of the blame, even if they acted in good faith. But, as we said in a previous chapter, the Wall Street boom was not the only cause of the crisis, which would have probably taken place in any case.

Producers all over the world, whether industrial or agricultural, also share the blame for the crisis. Individually they can hardly be held responsible for it, as none of them, except perhaps the very large combines, were in a position to form an idea as to the absorbing capacity of their markets. This ignorance was largely due to lack of co-operation between them. If they had pooled their statistical knowledge, and had kept each other informed about their respective plans, much overproduction could have been avoided. It is this failure to co-operate which is mainly responsible for the economic disequilibrium that brought about the crisis. There are a great many factors which have contributed to hasten, accentuate, or prolong it, but all of them pale into insignificance as compared with this cause. All evil tendencies which were at work could have been checked by means of co-operation. In various countries, short-sighted politicians, industrialists, financiers, and trade union leaders are to blame to some extent. We have seen that Soviet activities have also contributed to the troubles, but the main cause is the absence of adequate co-operation.

We have seen in previous chapters that the fact that the crisis developed into a spectacular panic was due to the concerted action between banks and Governments, and also to the improvement of international co-operation. We have tried to prove that the crisis could be brought nearer to its end by improving the existing means of collaboration. It follows that if in future we want to avoid a recurrence of the crisis, we shall have to develop a system in which co-operation of every kind plays a much more important part than it did in our pre-war system.

The importance of this is not sufficiently realised. Many people may think that because we were comparatively happy before the war, in spite of our periodical crises, there is no reason why we should not be happy again for ever, in spite of recurring temporary troubles. According to one school of thought, it is impossible to imagine an even progress of mankind. If there is to be any progress at all, they say, it has to be spasmodic and followed by natural reactions. It is worth our while to suffer occasional crises as we are more than rewarded by periods of prosperity, and, on balance, mankind is better off at the conclusion of every trade cycle. These arguments might carry conviction but for the fact that our economic and social system is no longer the only possible alternative. During the last fourteen years another system has developed, based on fundamentally different principles to those of our system. If, within the next few decades, it becomes evident that the Communist experience in Soviet Russia is successful, and that it is capable of providing the large masses of the population with a higher standard of living than that of capitalist countries, then our political, economic, and social system is doomed.

It is time to realise that we are running the greatest race in history, and that in the long run the principle of the survival of the fittest will prevail. At the present moment the Communist system still lags far behind ours. In spite of our present crisis, the average standard of living in capitalist countries is higher than that of the Soviet Union. The question is whether we shall be able to maintain our superiority. It would be a mistake to minimise the progress made in Soviet Russia during the last few years. We have no exact or even approximate knowledge of the situation. Most of the information that we receive is prejudiced either in favour or against the Soviet system, but the fact remains that, notwithstanding the enormous initial difficulties they had to cope with, the system still exists and is making progress. In fact, there is good reason to assume that, if the progress of Soviet Russia is maintained at the same rate as during the last few years, and if the capitalist world does not improve on its record of the last few decades, our superiority may gradually disappear during the lifetime of the present generation. Of course it cannot be taken for granted that the progress of the Communist system will continue on its present basis. We have seen in the course of history that countries with vast undeveloped resources make spectacular strides in the early stages of their development, but later they reach a stage when progress gradually slows down, and eventually they may even reach a state of stagnation. Russia possesses vast natural resources, and there is an immense scope for their development. The present Communistic experiment is entirely without precedent, and it is impossible to prophesy how far it will be able to proceed before its development will reach its zenith. Possibly it will be before they have caught us up, but we cannot build our hopes upon that. We cannot afford to depend on the weakness of our opponents. It is of vital importance that we should throw all our strength into the race.

Should the Soviet Union pursue an aggressive and destructive export policy, the rest of the world may be compelled into a defensive alliance which would have to make use of the weapon of economic boycott. It is possible, however, that the Soviet authorities realise that there is no hope for stirring up a world revolution

by means of ruining the industries of capitalist countries through cut-throat competition. In that case they
focus all their energies upon trying to accentuate their
economic progress instead of trying to destroy that of
other countries. Our task will then be to do our utmost
to maintain and even increase our economic superiority
over the new system.

To that end it is essential that we should establish co-operation in all its possible forms. We cannot
afford any longer to suffer periodical set-backs caused
by crises. It is explained in Appendix VI. that
the world crisis left Soviet Russia practically unaffected; should we undergo a few more such crises,
it would be a highly effective propaganda against
the capitalist system. The rival economic interests
which are reluctant to curtail their freedom of
action for the sake of co-operation should be made
aware that their very existence is at stake. Nothing
but the closest relations between them, coupled with
the co-operation of political powers to maintain
internal and international peace, can maintain the
superiority of our economic system which is the
raison d'être of our social and political system. In
order to accelerate our progress and to prevent set-
backs, individuals, groups, and classes will have to
consent to sacrifices which will be, however, rewarded
in the long run by the results obtained. If we combine
judiciously the advantages of co-operation with those
of individual initiative, there is no reason to fear that
a system where individual initiative is eliminated can
ever win the victory over us.

K

APPENDICES

APPENDIX I

CONDITIONS in Great Britain had been difficult already before the world crisis. While other countries succeeded in recovering from the post-war slump, Great Britain continued to suffer from chronic industrial depression without interruption throughout the post-war period. Although there was considerable improvement in trade conditions between 1922 and 1929, the number of unemployed remained above one million. Thus, while business houses and individuals in foreign countries succeeded in accumulating substantial reserves during the period of prosperity, in Great Britain the accumulation of wealth during that period was moderate. When the world crisis broke, some of the causes responsible operated in England to a particularly great extent, and, moreover, there were a number of causes peculiar to this country which tended to accentuate the crisis.

It cannot be said that there was overproduction in Great Britain in a sense of the output surpassing the actual demand for it. The depressed industries worked below their capacity during several years. On the other hand, there certainly was a considerable amount of underconsumption. Although the unemployed received the dole, which many think to have erred on the side of excessive generosity, the total spending power of the country could not but be affected by prolonged unemployment. At the same time signs of overconsumption were to some extent noticeable as far as the employed classes were concerned. Although the system of instalment buying has not reached the same proportions as in the United States, it tended to become increasingly popular. The fact that, while export trade was bad, the stores were crowded with

133

buyers, seems to indicate that the factors which supported domestic purchasing power were by no means negligible.

Post-war Great Britain provided a characteristic example of the country where economic conditions were slow to adjust themselves to changed conditions. Certain branches of production enjoyed prosperity, and there was a considerable amount of building activity. On the other hand, the three principal industries, namely, iron and steel, coal, and textile, suffered from chronic depression. It became obvious that they had lost for ever part of their foreign markets as a result of the industrialisation of foreign countries; up to now the greater part of the unemployed of these industries has not been absorbed by other industries.

The monetary causes of the crisis played a prominent part in Great Britain. As London was practically the only free gold market in Europe, she had to stand the full burden of French gold purchases. At the same time the high money rates in New York during the Wall Street boom diverted a considerable portion of foreign balances from London to New York. As a result the Bank of England had to raise its bank rate to 6½ per cent in September 1929, and it was by no means certain whether even this rate would be sufficient to safeguard the bank's gold reserve. This rising tendency of the bank rate was largely responsible for the liquidation on the Stock Exchange popularly attributed to the Hatry crisis. There is no doubt that there was a considerable amount of overspeculation also in London. While in New York overspeculation was to a certain extent justified by the period of prosperity of the United States, in London it lacked any such justification. Speculation manifested itself, apart from the rise in the price of shares of genuine industrial enterprises, in a reckless and unreasonable demand on the part of the public for shares of doubtful companies promoted by the hundred during the boom period. Unquestionably this boom accelerated the advent of the crisis, and had a substantial share in delaying recovery, for the disappointed and impoverished public is now reluctant to take an interest in any kind of investment.

Soviet dumping had no direct effect upon Great Britain, for

it confined itself mainly to goods which this country in any case must buy from abroad, and for this reason it was of positive advantage to be able to buy them cheaper. It had, however, an indirect effect upon British trade, inasmuch as it reduced the willingness and capacity of some of our best customers to buy British goods. To give only one example, ever since their existence the Swedish State Railways had bought their coal supply in Great Britain. As a result of the reduction of the price of Polish-Upper Silesian coal, made possible by indirect Government subsidy, the State Railways transferred their orders to Polish coal producers. Considering that Great Britain has always been the principal market for Swedish timber, it might have been possible to come to terms with the Swedish Government to disregard the difference in price and to continue to buy British coal. As, however, the reduction in the price of Polish coal coincided with the loss of the British market for Swedish timber in consequence of the dumping of Soviet timber, the Swedish Government could not be expected to make any sacrifice in the interest of Anglo-Swedish trade relations.

The slump in silver has affected Great Britain to a greater extent than any other industrial country. Because India is the best customer of British textiles, the reduction of the purchasing power of the Indian population was bound to react upon conditions in this country.

Apart from the factors which operated all over the world, and in which, as we have seen above, Great Britain had her due share, there were a number of individual adverse factors. The Socialist victory at the General Election of 1929 was one of these factors. This is not the place to consider the merits or demerits of the late Socialist Government or the shortcomings of political parties in general. Let it be sufficient to point out that, from a purely economic point of view, the advent of a Labour Government on the eve of the world crisis was decidedly disadvantageous, and that their continued rule throughout 1930 and 1931 largely contributed to accentuate the depression. As the declared aim of the Socialist Government is to shift the greater part of the burden of the country upon the wealthy classes, the result of their policy was naturally a wholesale emigration of capital and the discouragement of enterprise in Great Britain. Fear of higher direct taxation and other anti-capitalist measures have discouraged industrialists, while the efflux of capital considerably aggravated the exchange situation. In individual branches of industries the declared intention of Mr. Snowden to abolish safeguarding and McKenna duties resulted in a reduction of activity. The presence of a Socialist Government, moreover, encouraged the working classes to resist to the utmost any attempt to reduce wages in Great Britain to a basis that would make British costs competitive. This, together with the abuse of the system of doles and with the excessive strength of trade unions, has effectively prevented the readjustment of the cost of production in England to that of foreign countries. While the fall in prices was followed in almost every country by a reduction of wages, in Great Britain, owing to these circumstances, the wage level remained practically unaffected. Thus, while the fall of prices in other countries brought them nearer a return to prosperity, in Great Britain it tended to make conditions more difficult as the discrepancy between the wage level in this country and the wage level abroad tended to become greater.

The existence of a system of Free Trade has also contributed to accentuate the crisis. It is beyond the scope of this book to discuss the respective advantages of Free Trade and Protection in general, but it is obvious that Protection can certainly provide temporary relief to trade in prolonged periods of depression. In other countries, by the introduction of new customs duties and the increase of the existing ones, the domestic market has been preserved for domestic production to an even greater extent than was the case before. British industries and agriculture, however, received no such relief.

Another factor peculiar to Great Britain was the decline of confidence abroad in the stability of sterling. As a result of the persistent drain of gold due to the French demand and the refusal of the Bank of France to accept gold of standard fineness, foreign holders of sterling balances began to show signs of uneasiness, and towards the end of 1930 they withdrew part of their balances. An improvement of sterling at the beginning of 1931 and the establishment of better relations with the French monetary authorities have succeeded, temporarily, in restoring confidence, and some of the balances have returned to earn the higher interest rates offered in the London market.

The crisis reached its climax in Great Britain in the summer of 1931. The banking difficulties in Central Europe raised doubts as to the resisting capacity of London, and foreign holders of sterling balances in London began to withdraw their funds in great haste. In the course of July the Bank of England lost some £32,000,000 of gold, and on August 1 it announced that a credit of £50,000,000 had been granted by the French and American monetary authorities. As the wholesale withdrawal of funds continued, this credit soon proved to be inadequate to safeguard the stability of sterling. After the formation of the National Government, which undertook to balance the budget at the price of heavy sacrifices, a second credit of £80,000,000 was concluded by the British Treasury, but even this credit was inadequate to meet the pressure. By September 21 its proceeds were completely used up, and the authorities had no other course than to suspend the gold standard. The immediate result was a depreciation of sterling by some 30 per cent. In October there was a partial recovery owing to uncertainty as to the position of other currencies, but in November and December sterling resumed its downward trend. The protectionist measures introduced by the new Government, after it had received an overwhelming majority at the General Election, had no immediate effect upon sterling. Nevertheless, since the suspension of the gold standard there have been signs of a moderate trade revival. As a result of the depreciation of sterling British exporters have been able to compete more effectively in overseas markets, and have succeeded in gaining some ground in spite of the additional customs duties and exchange restrictions introduced by many countries. Unemployment for some months showed a slow decline. There were signs to indicate that the working classes had realised the necessity for adjusting wages and working hours to the requirements of the situation.

Towards the end of December sterling underwent a marked recovery, which continued and became accentuated in January 1932. The authorities were thus able to acquire the exchanges necessary for the repayment of the outstanding balances of the Bank of England's Franco-American credit falling due on January 31. What is more, they were even in a position during February to repay in advance a great part of the Treasury's Franco-American credit, which was not due until the end of August. The budgetry outlook has also improved considerably, thanks to economies and increased receipts from income-tax and Customs duties. There was also a decidedly better tendency in trade. Money rates declined, and the bank rate was gradually reduced from 6 per cent to 2 per cent. The improvement of trade was not, however, of a lasting character. From April onwards, unemployment began to increase once more. It appeared that the advantages gained through the depreciation of sterling had become largely counteracted by the sharp fall of prices abroad, by the depreciation of other currencies, and by the increase of Customs tariffs and other restrictions against imports introduced by a number of countries. Owing to the slackness of trade the low money rates were unable to bring about an increased demand for credit.

The solidity of the British business world in general and of the banking system in particular has been one of the few bright spots during the crisis. Although the wave of business failures did not avoid this country, their number and extent was, comparatively speaking, smaller than in most foreign countries. The reason for this is the sound traditions of British business and the very effective support received from British banks, who were willing to carry their customers through a difficult period, even at a cost of risk and sacrifice. Although there were a few isolated bank failures towards the end of 1929, the houses concerned were insignificant and their disappearance was not regretted. The British banking system as a whole displayed an amazing resisting capacity against adverse tendencies, and throughout the crisis enjoyed the full confidence of the British public.

APPENDIX II

THE United States is unique as the country where the crisis took place according to the classical rules of trade cycles. The post-war slump of 1920–1921 was succeeded there by a period of relative inactivity, which again was followed by a gradual improvement. In 1926 and 1927 the country began to enjoy a period of great prosperity, which gave rise to a wave of optimism. The American public is always inclined to exaggerate everything, and trade tendencies are by no means an exception to this rule. It was widely, almost generally, believed that prosperity would last for ever and would go on increasing. The origin of this belief was the accumulation of a huge gold stock during and after the war. The natural wealth of the United States is a matter of common knowledge, and the comparative lack of financial resources was, before the war, the main obstacle to their better exploitation. By the possession of a huge gold reserve and an improved credit system it was hoped that all these resources could be turned to the benefit of the nation in the course of the next decade or two. With her population of some 130 millions, protected by a high tariff, the United States provided an excellent market well insulated from fluctuations of demand abroad. Once a debtor nation, the United States has become a big creditor nation, and European Governments, as well as private borrowers, will have to contribute large amounts to the national income year after year for decades to come.

In such circumstances it is easy to understand the optimism of the American public. This optimism was encouraged rather than discouraged by leading bankers and statesmen, and it was largely responsible for the popularisation of instalment buying. Everybody expected to have a share in the increasing prosperity, and considered it permissible, therefore, to spend in advance part of this anticipated increase. Selling on instalment terms assumed dangerous dimensions all over the United States. Though part of it was directed to the acquisition of houses and other objects of lasting value, a great part of it was spent on luxuries and perishable goods. The demand created by instalment buying stimulated an extension of the productive capacity of American industries to an abnormally great extent.

The increasing tendency of the earnings of business concerns was largely responsible for the boom and overspeculation in Wall Street. In the opinion of many American authorities, the reduction of the New York bank rate in October 1927 was the cause of the boom, but this view appears rather one-sided and exaggerated. When the American public wants to speculate, considerations of interest rate play a quite subordinate part. The reduction of the rediscount rate stimulated speculation undoubtedly by means of further encouraging the optimism of the public, but its effect should not be overestimated. As a result of the Stock Exchange boom, which lasted approximately two years, immense fictitious wealth was created. Millions of people participated in it. This fictitious wealth contributed to increase spending still further, and increased spending, in its turn, accentuated the wave of prosperity. It seemed as if nothing would ever break this vicious circle. And yet the situation was becoming increasingly dangerous, and the comparatively small disturbance of the stock markets occasioned by the Hatry crisis in London was sufficient to bring about the collapse which was already long overdue. The violent slump and the subsequent period of decline in Wall Street destroyed immense fictitious values and reduced the capacity and the inclination of the American public to spend. Instalment buying died away, as people found it hard to pay for goods already in use. The earnings of business concerns were, therefore, bound to suffer. The decline of commodity prices, which had become noticeable a few months before the Wall Street crash, became more rapid, and industrial and commercial firms had to write off huge amounts on account of the depreciation of their stocks of raw materials. The agricultural crisis also affected conditions in the United States, which, in spite of the rapid progress of industrialisation, has remained a fundamentally agricultural country.

A circumstance tending to aggravate the situation was the peculiar banking position. It is an open secret that many of the American banks have to carry large amounts of securities as a result of the inability of their customers to sell them at prices sufficiently high to repay the sums they have borrowed from their banks. But for the efficiently organised Federal Reserve System and the mutual support granted by the large banks to each other, a general disaster would have been inevitable. As it is, most banks have successfully withstood the run of November and December 1930. Although a number of small banks in the South and Middle West suspended payment, the banking system as a whole displayed a good power of resistance.

The inclination of the American character to exaggerate everything was largely responsible for the accentuation of the crisis. While the public was exaggerated in its optimism, it is now equally exaggerated in its pessimism.

The desperate efforts of strong financial interests to check the downward trend on the Stock Exchange contributed to the prolongation of the crisis. Although their moderating influence upon the slump prevented it from degenerating into a panic, it is open to question whether, taking the long view, their action was beneficial to the United States and to the world in general. Their resources were not strong enough to bolster up stock prices at a level unjustified by business conditions and prospects, in face of the persistent selling pressure of the public. Although the temporary rallies they succeeded in provoking from time to time enabled some of them to unload part of their holding, in the long run the effect of their efforts was merely to delay the decline of security prices to a level at which they could attract once more the genuine investor.

Although American banks were heavily involved in the Central European banking crisis, it was not until after the suspension of the gold standard in Great Britain that the United States began to feel the effects of the aggravation of the crisis in Europe. There was a run on a number of small and medium-sized banks, and the number of failures attained unprecedented figures. This caused the hoarding of notes amounting to some $360,000,000. At the same time anxiety over the position of the Federal Reserve System caused the withdrawal of gold by foreign countries to the amount of over $700,000,000. As the major part of the withdrawals of gold was due to French action, the American authorities considered it necessary to come to terms with the French authorities; at the price of political and financial concessions the latter have agreed to leave their balances in New York. The result of this agreement has been the restoration of confidence in the dollar, and the efflux of gold has ceased. Bank failures have become fewer, thanks to the return of confidence and to the work of the National Credit Co-operation, established with the support of the strong to help the weak banks.

During the first half of 1932 there was from time to time a flight from the dollar, which brought the exchanges above gold export point, and the Federal Reserve Bank lost considerable amounts of gold. The adverse trend was largely due to the repatriation of foreign Central Bank balances, though to some extent there were signs also of a reflux of American capital. It was not until the beginning of June that the repatriation of foreign Central Bank balances was practically completed, and that confidence in the stability of the dollar definitely returned. The depression of business conditions continued unabated, and by June the number of unemployed was estimated at ten millions. A variety of schemes have been put forward in financial and political circles for raising the price level, but so far the actual steps taken in that direction have met with no success. The banking situation changed for the worse in June, when a number of banks in Chicago and elsewhere closed their doors.

APPENDIX III

It was not until the second half of 1930 that the world-wide depression began to make itself felt in France. Several reasons contributed to delay its repercussion in that country. In the first place, the stabilisation of the franc was carried out in circumstances which provided an artificial stimulus to French trade for several years. The rate of 124·21 francs to the pound did not correspond to the internal purchasing power of the franc, which was considerably higher. The process of the readjustment of the French price level to the world level was very slow, and was, to some extent, delayed by the official monetary policy, which aimed at preventing the influx of gold from producing its full effect in the form of expansion of the note circulation. France was, therefore, in a favourable position to compete in the world markets, and this accounts for the steady exports surplus she enjoyed until the end of 1930. Owing to the slowly rising trend of her price level, her internal trade activity also received a moderate stimulus.

The work provided by the reconstruction of the devastated areas helped French industries to modernise their plants. Although the work was practically completed some years ago, its beneficial effect upon French industries was of a lasting nature. The increase of tourist traffic provided an additional source of prosperity. Some years ago the French Riviera was discovered as a summer resort, and during the last few years France has had practically a twelve-months tourist season. As a result of prosperity in the United States and other countries, the hundreds of thousands of visitors who came year after year to France spent freely, and the French hotel industry and luxury trades experienced a prosperity without precedent.

The successful stabilisation of the franc and the subsequent accumulation of a huge gold reserve and foreign exchange reserve created a wave of optimism in France. This optimism was, however, better founded and more moderate than that of the American public. It did not lead to a speculative boom, but assisted in the consolidation of the progress of industries attained during the period of inflation and reconstruction. As a result of the stabilisation of the franc at one-fifth of its pre-war value, debts contracted for reconstruction purposes had been written down by four-fifths of their nominal value, so that the burden was no longer excessive; on the other hand, Germany was making substantial payments which, after the completion of the work of reconstruction, could be used for debt redemption and for the creation of external reserves.

Another reason why France resisted the crisis longer than almost any other country was exceptional self-sufficiency. Although she has developed into an industrial country, her agriculture is nevertheless in a position to produce the greater part of her food requirements. Because she need not import, she relies less upon exports. Thus her prosperity does not depend to such an extent on that of foreign countries as, for example, does that of Great Britain.

In spite of all this, the depression began to make itself felt to an increasing extent in the course of 1930. The export of French luxury articles was affected by the Wall Street slump and the subsequent world-wide depression which diminished the purchasing power of many of her best customers. For the same reason, tourist traffic declined considerably; even those who could afford to spend a holiday in France were much more careful in their expenditure than they used to be before the crisis. The slump in agricultural produce affected the rural population, while the wine-producing areas were affected by the bad vintage of 1930 in addition to the fall of prices.

As a result of all these factors, unemployment began to increase during the second half of 1930. Although no reliable statistics are available, it is believed to have passed the million mark well before the end of that year. To some extent the increase of unemployment was delayed by the gradual reduction of foreign workmen employed in France. Until 1930 the French authorities pursued an extremely liberal policy towards the immigration of foreign labour. There was ample employment for everybody, and, owing to the stagnation of the French population, the authorities considered it desirable to encourage the immigration of elements which were likely to assimilate with the French nation in the course of a generation. Most of these workmen obtained temporary permits, which were renewable from time to time. When unemployment began to increase, all the French authorities had to do was to decline to renew permits, and thereby the foreign workmen were gradually compelled to leave France.

While the depression was comparatively moderate until the autumn of 1930, in October last it suddenly led to a banking crisis. As a result of the collapse of the Oustric group, the French public, which is none too trustful by nature, began to withdraw their deposits, not only from small provincial banks, but even from the largest Paris commercial banks. The latter, of course, found it easy to resist the pressure, but a number of small and medium-sized banks in Paris and the provinces were compelled to suspend payment. After the turn of the year the banking crisis gradually subsided, and the deposits withdrawn were returned. At the same time the experience of the last quarter of 1930 has made France realise that she cannot remain prosperous amidst a world-wide depression. It is probably owing to this consideration that, as from the beginning of 1931, the French authorities showed an increased willingness to co-operate in the international sphere.

As a result of the fall of world prices, the discrepancy between wholesale prices in France and in other countries has disappeared almost completely. But for this fall, it might have taken years before French prices rose to the world level. As it were, the world level declined to the vicinity of the French price level. In consequence, the advantageous position of French export trade, which existed ever since the war, has practically ceased, and the trade balance turned against France.

L

At the same time retail prices continued to rise, in spite of the fall of wholesale prices, and by the end of 1930 France ceased to be a cheap country for tourists.

The Central European banking crisis affected France to a comparatively small extent, as her authorities have discouraged French banks from lending to Germany and to other countries in Central Europe. On the other hand, the suspension of the gold standard in Great Britain created an acute bank crisis in France. There was a run on a number of banks, including the Banque Nationale de Crédit, which had to be saved by official support. A number of other banks were less fortunate, because the authorities have apparently adopted the policy of supporting only the biggest banks. Several important failures occurred both in Paris and in the provinces. The hoarding habit of the public assumed fantastic dimensions, as was indicated by the spectacular increase of the note circulation. The position of the Bank of France itself gave rise to uneasiness; it was generally known that the Bank of France held substantial sterling balances, and its losses upon these balances through the depreciation of sterling were estimated to exceed its total capital and reserves several times over. To reassure the public the French Government has agreed to take over the losses of the Bank of France.

The economic situation became considerably worse during the second half of 1931. The demand for French luxury exports declined, and those branches of industries which depend on these exports were seriously affected. There was also a heavy decline of tourist traffic owing to the depreciation of sterling, the crisis in Central Europe and the United States, and to the revival of economic nationalism in various countries.

The banking situation has improved considerably since the turn of the year. The wave of bank failures has ceased almost completely, and the volume of hoarding showed a declining tendency. With the increase of the Bank of France's gold reserve, confidence in the stability of the franc has been restored, though the public is still prepared to pay a premium on gold coins. The budgetry situation gave rise to some concern, for it was obvious that the balancing of the Budget was purely artificial.

APPENDIX IV

THE economic crisis in Germany was not preceded by a boom or even by a period of prosperity. The short period of boom that followed the depression of 1924–1926, brought about by the stabilisation of the currency, collapsed in 1927. As American lending practically ceased in 1928 and 1929, the country suffered a lean period; interest rates were still abnormally high and capital was scarce. The uncertainty as to the solution of the problem of Reparations was still hanging over Germany's head. In 1929 the threatened collapse of the Paris conference of Reparation experts brought about a flight from the reichsmark. Though it was soon checked by means of heavy gold exports, it showed that confidence in the stability of the reichsmark was by no means as well established as was generally assumed.

Thus conditions were far from satisfactory at the moment of the Wall Street slump. As a result of the world-wide depression, German exports suffered to no slight extent. Another factor which contributed to aggravate the crisis was—strange as it may sound—the progress of rationalisation in German industries. Although, in the long run, it is bound to be beneficial to Germany, its immediate effect was a considerable increase of unemployment. Owing to the bad state of trade, the rationalised enterprises were not in a position to benefit immediately by their improved competitive capacity. As the advantages of rationalisation do not fully manifest themselves unless the plants are employed to a fairly great extent, for the present the results of rationalisation have proved to be unfavourable. An attempt has been made to induce the working classes to agree to a reduction of wages in proportion to the fall of prices; the agreements arrived at, however, failed to work to the satisfaction of all parties, and the attempts to reduce wages led to strikes in several branches of production.

German agriculture, which was none too prosperous, suffered considerably through the crisis, especially as a result of the dumping of Soviet grain. In order to safeguard the interests of the rural population, import duties have been re-established on agricultural products. It has been realised in Germany that, as it is difficult to find markets for manufactures, it is desirable to satisfy a great part of food and raw material requirements through an increase of the domestic agricultural production.

In addition to her economic troubles, Germany also underwent a political crisis in the autumn of 1930. The unexpected victory of the National Socialist Party created an atmosphere of uncertainty, as it was feared it would lead to internal disturbances and external complications, and in September and October 1930 there was a flight from the reichsmark; confidence was restored after a short time, as it was gradually realised that the victory of the National Socialists made little difference to the internal and international situation of Germany.

In a way, German industries have to some extent benefited by the crisis, inasmuch as the decline of money rates has enabled them to cover their requirements of working capital at a reasonable cost. They were not, however, in a position to take full advantage of this improvement, for their capital requirements have been considerably reduced as a result of the depression.

To some extent the suspension of the issue of external long-term loans was a blessing in disguise, as, at the rate Germany was borrowing abroad during 1925 to 1928, she would by now have increased her external indebtedness to an unbearable figure. As it is, she actually reduced her long-term indebtedness, for, owing to funds being more plentiful, a number of German debtors were able to repurchase a large part of their dollar bonds at advantageous prices. At the same time, however, Germany's external short-term indebtedness has increased. Large amounts of short deposits were received from France, and, whenever diplomatic relations become strained, there was a wholesale efflux of capital.

Unemployment in Germany attained staggering figures, and there was a record number of business failures. The uncertainty of the internal and external political situation—the fear of a National Socialist *coup d'État* and of a French aggression —was an additional factor tending to paralyse business activity. The emigration of capital, especially to Switzerland, assumed alarming dimensions towards the end of 1930. Early in 1931 conditions improved to some extent, but unemployment remained at a disquieting level, in spite of artificial stimulus of export trade by such means as the export credit granted to Soviet Russia under the guarantee of the German Government.

As a result of the strained international relations created by the Austrian Customs Union scheme, and of the wave of distrust aroused by the Creditanstalt affair, foreign banks began to withdraw funds from Germany on a large scale in May. The Reichsbank had to use up a large part of its gold and foreign exchange reserve, and received support from a group of central banks headed by the Bank for International Settlements. In spite of this the withdrawals threatened the stability of the Reichsmark. In July the situation became aggravated by a number of commercial failures, especially that of the Nordwolle, which resulted in a run on the Darmstädter- und National-Bank. On July 13 that bank suspended payment, and the Government introduced restrictions on payments by all banks in order to prevent a general run. These restrictions were gradually removed, and the German banks concluded a standstill agreement with their foreign creditors, according to which credits were prolonged until February 29. The Stock Exchange, which was closed on July 13, was reopened in September, but after a short time it had to be closed once more, and remained closed for the rest of the year. The depreciation of sterling brought some relief to Germany, by reducing in terms of gold the burden of certain German debts. At the same time it has increased the competitive capacity of British industries, and this, together with customs duties introduced in Great Britain and other countries, affected adversely German export trade.

Although Germany had a large export surplus, the pressure against the reichsmark continued because the greater part of the proceeds of the exports was left abroad. In November the Government applied to the Bank for International Settlements to appoint a committee in virtue of the Young Plan to investigate Germany's capacity to pay Reparations. Uncertainty as to the outcome of the coming Reparations conference, as well as the threat of violent internal political developments, tended to aggravate the economic situation.

The conclusion of a standstill agreement for twelve months has consolidated to some extent the situation. A drastic reconstruction of the leading banks has been carried out with the participation of the Government and the Reichsbank. From April onwards the favourable trade balance began to decline, and it was feared that should this adverse tendency continue it might become necessary to declare a transfer moratorium for all external debt payments. Economic conditions were becoming desperate, and it was only the hopes of an improvement as a result of the Lausanne Conference that prevented a collapse.

APPENDIX V

THE world crisis found Italy amidst conditions which were far from satisfactory. This was largely due to the mistake committed in stabilising the lira at a level which did not correspond to its internal purchasing power. While the stabilisation of the French franc at a too low value necessitated the rise of internal prices, the stabilisation of the lira at a too high value brought about a fall of the price level. It took several years for internal prices to readjust themselves to the new exchange value of the lira. Meanwhile export industries were severely handicapped in international competition.

Fortunately for Italy, she does not possess any substantial raw material resources. This is a paradox, for in normal conditions this circumstance is a great disadvantage; but during a period of decline in raw material prices this proved to be a blessing; for, in addition to industrial depression caused by the mistaken stabilisation of the lira, the country would have had to suffer also through the depreciation of her raw material assets, and the crisis would have assumed almost intolerable dimensions.

Already before the beginning of the world crisis Italy was suffering from depression. From time to time there were commercial failures of considerable importance, and a large number of small banks disappeared through failure or liquidation. At the same time Italy had the great advantage of being ruled by dictatorship—a very useful institution for times of crises—which had the means of bringing about a compulsory adjustment of wages and prices to the new level. While in

151

Germany attempts to bring about an agreement between employers and employees for an all-round reduction of wages did not bring the desired result, and while in Great Britain no general attempt has even been made to that end, in Italy all wages, salaries, etc., have been reduced overnight by decree, simultaneously with a corresponding reduction in various items of the cost of living. But for the possibility of such forced readjustment, the position in Italy would have become considerably aggravated.

The industrial depression could not but affect the banking situation in Italy. Banks and industries are closely associated in almost every country on the Continent, but whereas in most countries this association assumes the form of a control of industries by banks, in Italy, on the other hand, banks are largely under the control of industrial interests. This is obviously an undesirable state of affairs, as those in control are naturally inclined to use the banks' resources for the financing of their own enterprises to a dangerous extent. This was the case of the Banca Agricola Italiana, which was controlled by Signor Gualino, who lent the major part of the bank's funds to his own enterprises. The result was that the bank had to be liquidated after the intervention of the authorities. The atmosphere thus created provided an opportunity for an attack directed against one of the leading banks. As a result of the circulation of a pamphlet criticising that bank, there were heavy withdrawals of deposits, but the bank faced the pressure without much difficulty and confidence was soon restored. At the same time the authorities and banking interests have learned a lesson, and it appears that efforts are now being made to divorce banking control and industrial interests.

As in the case of France and Germany, the political factor contributes to aggravate the crisis. Although the internal political situation is more stable than in any other European country, the international relations of Italy leave much to be desired. From time to time war scares create uneasiness, which is anything but helpful from the point of view of economic progress. Owing to the difficulty of obtaining independent information as to the conditions in Italy, that country is regarded abroad with a certain distrust, which tends to discourage the inflow of short-term capital.

The iron discipline enforced by the Fascist régime in every sphere of economic life has certainly contributed to reduce the number of failures. Owing to the severe penalties inflicted upon those who are responsible for failures, financiers and company promoters do their utmost to keep their companies alive. The authorities also compel banking interests to take over banks which would otherwise fail, even at the price of sacrifice. Notwithstanding this, there have been several failures of considerable importance during the past year.

Italy is greatly affected by the crisis in the United States, not only through a falling off of tourist traffic, but also through a severe decline in emigrants' remittances. Owing to bad economic conditions in the South American countries, which absorbed the greater part of Italian emigration since the war, the number of emigrants has declined, and this has also contributed to increase unemployment.

The Central European crisis affected the Italian banking situation to a relatively moderate extent only. Italian banks were neither large debtors nor creditors to German banks, although they had fairly substantial commitments in other Central European countries. The depreciation of sterling in September brought a pressure on the lira, as it was generally expected that Italy would follow the British example in suspending the gold standard. The Italian authorities have, however, successfully resisted the pressure, and have maintained the stability of the lira. While the international situation left the Italian banking situation comparatively unaffected, internal developments tended to aggravate the position. On the insistence of the Government the large Italian banks had to undertake to support the market in their own shares as well as commercial and industrial enterprises in which they were associated. As a result, they gradually acquired the bulk of the share capital of all those companies, and had to carry these holdings either directly or through the intermediary of their holding companies. This immobilised the banks to a great extent, and it became necessary to relieve them of their securities. Early in 1931 the Credito

Italiano was relieved of its securities and holdings by the authorities, while in November arrangements were made for relieving the Banca Commerciale Italiano of its frozen holdings. To that end a new institution has been formed, which is to issue debentures under Government guarantee.

In spite of the decline of emigrants' remittances, which, together with receipts from tourist traffic, constitute normally the greater part of the invisible exports, the stability of the lira has been maintained. Although economic conditions are unsatisfactory, the extent of unemployment is much smaller than in any of the leading countries. This may be attributed to the great extent of Government interference with economic life, as a result of which the adjustment of prices takes place in Italy quicker than anywhere else. The Government has also undertaken extensive public works, such as land-draining, etc., to mitigate unemployment.

APPENDIX VI

UNTIL the beginning of 1931 the Scandinavian countries succeeded in maintaining a comparatively high degree of prosperity. Although Denmark is an agricultural country, she does not produce any grain for export, but specialises in the production of butter, cheese, bacon, and other articles which were not affected by the crisis to the same extent as grain. As Great Britain is the principal market for Danish products, Denmark was among the first countries to follow the British example in suspending the gold standard. The atmosphere of uncertainty prevailing in October resulted in a run on one of the leading banks, but the public was soon reassured. As a result of import restrictions by a number of countries, and of a strike in the bacon industry, the Danish authorities had to introduce severe exchange restrictions. Efforts have been made to increase imports from Great Britain, so as to strengthen the case in favour of maintaining the British market for Danish products.

Norway had her crisis after the stabilisation of the exchange, and most of the weak banks and business enterprises were then eliminated. Those which survived were able to face the present depression. The situation of shipping and of the whaling industry are the two weakest points in Norway's economic situation. Idle tonnage attained record figures for the post-war period, while the increased output of whale oil, brought about by the employment of a tanker fleet, coinciding with lessened demand from the margarine and soap industries, resulted in a disastrous slump in the price. Together with the other Scandinavian countries Norway had to abandon the gold standard, and her currency moved for a while in sympathy with sterling.

In 1932, however, the Norwegian exchange, together with the Swedish krone, depreciated in relation to sterling.

Sweden remained remarkably prosperous until the end of 1930. Most of her banks succeeded in maintaining their profits and dividends, and some of her leading industrial enterprises continued to expand. Soviet dumping of timber in foreign markets, on the other hand, affected Sweden to no little extent. The slackening of demand for iron ore was also an adverse factor. On the other hand, the glass and other industries engaged in the production of specialities, the market for which has not yet reached saturation point, made further progress. The German crisis affected Sweden to a great extent, not merely because Swedish banks granted comparatively substantial credits to Germany, but also because it resulted in a wholesale repatriation of Swedish securities placed abroad during the last few years. As a result, the gold and foreign exchange reserves of the Riksbank declined rapidly. As attempts to raise a credit abroad failed, Sweden had to follow Great Britain in abandoning the gold standard. The crisis in Sweden attained its climax in March 1932 with the collapse of the Kreuger and Toll group. It appears that for the past twelve months or so that group received extensive support from the Riksbank and the Scandinaviska Kreditaktiebolaget. The collapse of the group has made it necessary to provide for the support of the latter. On the whole, Sweden has weathered the storm remarkably well. There were no bank failures, and the Riksbank was able to withstand the adverse trend against the krone.

Finland and the other Baltic states were also affected by Soviet dumping of timber and agricultural products. There were some bank failures both in Latvia and Estonia. Considering, however, the scarcity of capital and the initial difficulties with which these countries had to struggle, it may be said that they have withstood creditably a test of extreme severity. They were seriously affected by the German crisis, and also by the suspension of the gold standard in Great Britain. In October, Finland had to suspend the gold standard, while the three Baltic states remained nominally on a gold basis.

Poland's chief sources of national wealth are agriculture, coal, timber, textiles, and sugar. As all these branches were severely hit by the crisis, conditions were none too easy for her. In spite of this she stood the strain remarkably well until the beginning of 1931, when a series of banking and industrial failures occurred. The German crisis produced remarkably little effect in Poland. There have been no bank failures and no currency restrictions since May 1931, thanks to the financial assistance given by France for political purposes.

The economic crisis did not directly affect the position in Soviet Russia, as production and trade are artificially regulated and world tendencies have no direct effect upon them. The falling trend of world prices did not affect the internal price level in Soviet Russia, not only because prices are regulated there artificially, but also because the country is experiencing a new period of inflation, and those prices which are not fixed officially have an upward, rather than a downward, trend. Of course, the price of Soviet exports has fallen, but as the Government is the only exporter, the depreciation of its stocks did not cause any trouble to the owners.

Owing to the peculiar economic system adopted in the Soviet Union, there can be no crisis in the same sense as in countries with a capitalist economic system. This, however, does not mean that conditions in Soviet Russia are in any way better than in the rest of the world. The argument that the Communist economic system is free from the plague of periodical crises can be easily answered by pointing out that, crisis or no crisis, the population of Soviet Russia is still worse off than in almost any other country. Their welfare is sacrificed in the interest of the Five Years Plan. Although the amount of food produced in Soviet Russia is amply sufficient to cover requirements, the Government exports a great part of the food required at home so as to be able to buy machinery abroad. Whatever the ultimate result of this policy may be, for the present it inflicts suffering upon the population to an extent entirely unknown in other countries.

The fall in the prices of agricultural products is calculated to cause delay in the realisation of the Five Years Plan. Although manufactures have also a declining trend, their decline lags far behind that of agricultural products and other export articles of the Soviet, such as timber and oil. Thus, in order to be able to buy the same amount of machinery, the Soviet Union has to export more than she would have to export otherwise. For this reason, forecasts from Soviet sources that the Five Years Plan will be completed in four years instead of five must be regarded with some doubt.

To some extent the Soviet Union has benefited by the crisis in various ways. They found it easier to obtain credits than at any time during their existence, because every country has become more anxious to sell its goods. There is reason to believe that they reduced their expenditure on propaganda abroad, in part because they realised the futility of their efforts and in part because they hope that, owing to the economic crisis, the capitalist world may collapse without any propaganda; to this extent Soviet dumping has replaced the weapon of propaganda. As propaganda represented a very important item in the budget of the Soviet Union, this tended to improve their budgetary situation.

As a result of the German crisis the renewal of credits granted by Germany has become more and more difficult. Other countries have become also increasingly reluctant to grant credits to the Soviet, and it was feared that as a result some of the outstanding Soviet credits might be defaulted. These fears proved, however, to be without foundation. The most serious blow to the Soviet was, however, the depreciation of sterling. During the last seven years it has been the practice of the Soviet to use the marked excess of sales to England over purchases from England to pay for imports from Germany, the United States, and many other countries. The depreciation of sterling has seriously reduced the gold value of this sterling surplus, because the Soviet have not been able to get a sufficient increase in the sterling price of goods sold in England to offset the decline in the value of sterling.

APPENDIX VII

THE CRISIS IN CENTRAL AND EASTERN EUROPE

ECONOMIC nationalism assumed greater proportions in the Succession States of the late Austrian-Hungarian Monarchy than any other part of the world. Each one of the Succession States endeavoured to become an independent economic unit, as self-sufficient as possible. To that end a large number of industrial enterprises had been established in Central and South-Eastern Europe. These enterprises could only exist under the protection of a customs tariff, and catered only for the internal market. As a result of the agricultural crisis, the absorbing capacity of the internal market declined considerably and the new industrial enterprises began to work at a loss. As most of them had no opportunity to accumulate reserves, they were unable to stand the test.

. Considering the adverse circumstances, the number and extent of failures in Central and Eastern Europe has not been alarming during the early stages of the crisis. This was due to the general improvement of credit conditions. While, until the end of 1929, funds were extremely scarce in every country, with the possible exception of Czechoslovakia, and exorbitant rates of interest had to be paid for external credits, owing to the world-wide plethora of short-term funds, the leading banks of these countries gradually found it easier to obtain credits on reasonable terms. Thus, in spite of the difficulties of these countries to issue long-term loans, they were able to meet a great part of their requirements by means of short-term credits. The Governments of several of them have resorted to short-term borrowing in anticipation of an improvement of conditions in the international loan market, which would enable them to issue their postponed loans. This has rendered their position highly vulnerable, and has been one of the causes of subsequent troubles.

Czechoslovakia is practically the only country in Central and Eastern Europe which exports manufactured goods on a large scale. She succeeded in maintaining her exports in several branches owing to her low cost of production. Being, however, one of the principal sugar-producing countries, she was affected to a great extent by the sugar crisis. The Austrian and German troubles produced some repercussions on the Czechoslovak banking situation. Thanks to French assistance, however, a panic has been averted. The introduction of Customs duties in Great Britain has dealt a severe blow upon the Czechoslovak glass and other export industries, but, on the whole, Czechoslovakia displayed a stronger resistance to the crisis than any other country in Central Europe.

In Austria conditions were none too prosperous even before the crisis. Unemployment was comparatively high and the trade balance was strongly adverse. The deficit on the balance of visible trade was met largely by the invisible export item represented by the spendings of foreign tourists. The decline of tourist traffic brought about by the crisis was, therefore, a hard blow to Austria. Conditions were going from bad to worse, and the crisis culminated in the difficulties of the Creditanstalt, the largest bank of the country. The Government undertook to guarantee the liabilities of the Creditanstalt, which constitutes extremely heavy burdens. A fair amount of foreign capital has been withdrawn from the country, and the difficulties of the Creditanstalt has aggravated the industrial situation. The Austrian banks have concluded a standstill agreement with their foreign creditors, and the Government has succeeded in obtaining some credits abroad. Although nominally the stability of the exchange has been maintained, the rate quoted has been purely artificial. Negotiations for the definite settlement of the Government's liabilities arising from its guarantee of the Creditanstalt's liabilities have failed so far to result in an agreement. In July 1932 an international loan to cover the immediate requirements of Austria was arranged under the auspices of the League. It was, nevertheless, necessary to establish a transfer moratorium pending the issue of the loan.

In Hungary, as in every other agricultural country, the fall in the price of agricultural products affected the economic situation to a great extent. The hopes of raising a big external loan for railway construction and other public works did not materialise owing to the unfavourable conditions in the international market. The only change for the better was the definite funding of the country's liabilities arising from the war, which eliminated the uncertainty which still plays such a prominent part in the case of Germany. The Creditanstalt crisis resulted in grave repercussions upon the Hungarian banking situation. There was a run on the Hungarian General Credit Bank, and the Government had to support it with the aid of external credits. Eventually the banks concluded a standstill agreement with their foreign creditors, while restrictions imposed upon exchange operations made it impossible for importers to pay for their goods. In December 1931 a transfer moratorium was declared.

Roumania experienced a severe banking crisis early in 1930. This was due to the too close association between banks and industrial enterprises. The resources of several banks were tied up in industrial and commercial participations, and the run of depositors found them highly unprepared. A number of provincial banks were allowed to fail, but one of the leading banks which was also attacked received support and survived the crisis. As the chief export articles of the country are grain, timber, and oil, Soviet dumping of these commodities in world markets affected the situation to a particularly great extent. The distrust caused by the Central European banking troubles did not leave Roumania unaffected. As French support was not forthcoming in good time, several important banks had to be allowed to fail. Among others the Banca Marmorosch Blank & Co. had to close its doors.

Difficulties in the timber trade were also the chief source of trouble to Yugo-Slavia. Prolonged negotiations for a large external loan, which would have enabled the country to stabilise

M

its currency, arrived at a conclusion in 1931. As a result of the Central European crisis the situation has become aggravated to such an extent that the Government was considering the declaration of a general moratorium. At the eleventh hour, however, it received assistance from France, and was able to carry on. It was, nevertheless, inevitable that several of the leading banks of the country should avail themselves of the right to postpone the repayment of their debts for a certain number of months.

In Bulgaria conditions were deteriorating as a result of the acute scarcity of capital. Fortunately for the country, tobacco is one of its chief export products, and as the tobacco trade suffered comparatively little during the early stages of the crisis, it provided the country with valuable assistance to survive the crisis. After the Central European crisis credit conditions became extremely stringent, and several important failures occurred. Negotiations have been initiated to obtain assistance from France, but without result. In April the Government introduced a partial transfer moratorium of its external debts.

Conditions in Greece have remained comparatively satisfactory. Until the second half of 1931 Greece had the advantage of the increase of her population through the settlement of refugees from Asia Minor. The new population proved to be an extremely valuable productive element, and their gradual establishment in their new homes brought about increased economic activity to the advantage of the country. Moreover, Greece was one of the few countries which was able to obtain loans for public works in spite of adverse conditions in the capital markets of the world. Greece was not particularly involved in the Central European crisis, but was affected by the depreciation of sterling, as the Bank of Greece held a great part of its reserves in London. Towards the end of 1931 the ill-advised effort to maintain the gold standard, together with the falling off of exports and emigrants' remittances, aggravated the condition of Greece. Early in 1932 the Government applied for a moratorium. As no agreement could be reached with the creditors, the service of the external debt was suspended.

APPENDIX VIII

THE CRISIS IN OTHER EUROPEAN COUNTRIES

THE prosperity of Holland depends largely upon that of her colonial empire. As a result of the boom in rubber and other colonial products, she experienced a period of great prosperity after the war. The slump in the prices of these products, and the resulting depression in the colonies, was bound to affect the situation in the mother-country unfavourably. The reason why the crisis was, comparatively speaking, not very severe in Holland was that Dutch people, as a rule, pursued a very conservative policy and possessed ample reserves to survive the lean period. The increase of German customs tariffs on agricultural products affected the country to some extent. Another adverse point was the crisis in the diamond trade, which plays an important part in Amsterdam. The country has also suffered through the decline of transit trade, which plays an important part in the traffic of the ports of Amsterdam and Rotterdam. The Dutch market was flooded with European dollar bonds issued in New York, but, in spite of that, Dutch banks were in a position to issue foreign loans even after the leading markets had suspended their international issuing activity. As Dutch banks have lent to Germany and other Central European countries to a great extent, they were bound to be affected by the Central European crisis. Thanks to the strong position of the Netherlands Bank, however, they were able to weather the storm. Towards the middle of September a severe slump occurred on the Amsterdam Stock Exchange, which has contributed to no slight extent to London's difficulties, as large blocks of arbitrage securities were unloaded in London. The depreciation of sterling inflicted heavy losses upon the Netherlands Bank, which considered it advisable to repatriate the greater part of its dollar balances in October.

Belgium is economically closely associated with France, and as the crisis did not produce its effect in France until the latter part of 1930, it did not affect Belgium until that time. In fact, Belgium was to a great extent at an advantage, even as compared with France. While the French franc was stabilised at 124, the Belgian franc was stabilised at 175. Prices were, therefore, considerably lower in Belgium than in France, and the stimulus to exports was even greater than in the case of France. In the late autumn of 1930 the crisis began to manifest itself by difficulties in the Belgian textile industries. The diamond crisis also affected Belgium, while the all-round decline of securities depreciated the considerable assets of Belgian holding companies. Already, before the Wall Street slump, the Brussels Bourse was rather depressed as a result of the Loewenstein crisis and of the collapse of the attempt to establish an international Cork Trust. The expansion of banking by means of amalgamations and capital increases, which was assuming spectacular dimensions during 1929, came to a sudden end. This was, however, to the advantage of the country, as the movement was rather overdone.

Luxembourg experienced a period of comparative prosperity notwithstanding the world-wide depression. As a result of the favourable treatment of foreign holding companies, hundreds of such companies were registered with the co-operation of the local banks, which underwent a remarkable expansion.

As Switzerland is largely dependent upon tourist traffic, the crisis was bound to affect her prosperity. Her special industries, such as, for instance, watch-making, were also affected, not merely by the general depression, but also by the increase in the American and other tariffs. At the same time Switzerland benefited to a great extent by the influx of foreign capital seeking refuge there from high taxation or from political or financial uncertainty. This influx assumed such dimensions that the banks had to take measures to discourage it. They ceased to pay interest on new deposits and in some cases even refused to accept accounts from new customers. They were faced with the problem of investing profitably the funds received. In some quarters it was feared that the plethora of funds might lead to a speculative boom and industrial overproduction; in reality, however, these fears failed to materialise. The mere fact that money is cheap and plentiful does not, in itself, induce manufacturers to extend their activities if they have no markets on which to place their surplus. As a result of excessive supplies of funds, the foreign loan market of Switzerland was rather active during 1930 and 1931. In fact, it may be said to have been the most active of all foreign loan markets. As capital was not particularly wanted for domestic purposes, public opinion —which, in the olden days, was strenuously opposed to foreign lending—ceased to raise any objection to this activity. The German crisis affected Switzerland to a comparatively greater extent than any other creditor country. The participation of Swiss banks in German credits was large in proportion to their resources, and this fact gave rise to considerable uneasiness as to the banks' position in the country. Fortunately, however, the Swiss National Bank, with its gold reserve of 160 per cent, was able to cope with the situation, and confidence was restored. There were a few bank failures, but the leading banks were unscathed, notwithstanding the withdrawal of German and other deposits. It was feared that the Kreuger crisis might produce grave repercussions upon the country, as Swiss banks and the public were involved to an unduly great extent. The storm has blown over, however, without any disastrous consequences.

In Spain the general economic depression was accentuated by the political uncertainty and by the fluctuation of the peseta. In spite of this, economic conditions were tolerable, presumably because of the depreciating currency, which gave trade a certain stimulus. The revolution of April 1931 brought about a change of régime which, for the time being, eliminated the source of uncertainty caused by the Republican movement. At the same time separatist endeavours in several parts of Spain continued to remain a source of political uncertainty, tending to aggravate the economic situation. Repeated attempts at the stabilisation of the currency have failed. In the summer of 1931 the Bank of Spain succeeded in obtaining a large loan from the Bank of France, but in spite of this the peseta continued to fluctuate owing to political troubles. Moreover, the depreciation of sterling inflicted heavy losses upon the Bank of Spain.

Portugal was affected by the depression in her colonies, which resulted in banking difficulties. Her political situation was also far from stable and was a source of uncertainty. Although the revolt in Madeira was suppressed, the possibility of further political troubles has added to the difficulties of the country. In June 1931 Portugal stabilised the escudo at the rate of 110 to sterling. When the gold standard was suspended in Great Britain the escudo remained stable in relation to sterling, and fluctuated proportionately in relation to other currencies. Thanks to the sound management of Portuguese finances, and to the timely decision to disconnect the exchange from gold, conditions in the country have remained comparatively prosperous.

APPENDIX IX

As the British Dominions and Colonies are essentially agricultural countries they were particularly affected by the crisis. In Canada the difficulties had already begun during the Wall Street boom, which diverted a considerable amount of Canadian funds to New York. Apart from the withdrawal of American funds invested in Canada, and the heavy buying of American shares, the flow of funds across the border was also due to abnormally high interest rates in Wall Street. The disadvantage of not possessing a money market of her own was clearly revealed. As in Canada there are no facilities for short-term investments in a liquid form, the banks and leading companies usually hold their balances in New York. These balances were considerably increased during the boom, when fantastic interest rates were being paid. As a result of the transfer of funds, the exchanges moved strongly against Canada, and she was eventually obliged temporarily to suspend the gold standard by unofficially reimposing the embargo on gold exports. Moreover, the financial resources of the country for trade purposes were depleted. After the Wall Street collapse the funds thus withdrawn were returned and the Canadian dollar rose to par again. The embargo on gold exports was removed, and the gold standard was thus once more restored. At the same time conditions were anything but happy : owing to the proximity of the United States the Canadian public took a particularly active part in speculation in Wall Street, and suffered, therefore, heavy losses through the collapse. The agricultural situation was also very grave. In no part of the world, except in the United States, has the use of harvesting machinery become so popular, and Canadian grain production increased to a considerable extent in consequence. The short-sighted policy of the Canadian wheat pool has also contributed to accentuate the losses inflicted upon the country by the decline of grain prices. On the assumption that the decline was of a purely temporary nature, the wheat pool held off its enormous supplies from the market for many months, and eventually it had to sell them at much lower prices. The suspension of the gold standard in Great Britain was followed by an increase in discount at which the Canadian exchange stood in relation to the U.S. dollar. The Dominion Government was, nevertheless, determined not to allow the Canadian dollar to follow the course of sterling. It failed, however, to keep it at par with the United States dollar, and, in spite of repeated declarations to the contrary, the gold standard had in practice to be abandoned. Since then the exchange has been fluctuating at approximately half-way between the pound and the United States dollar. Adverse rumours as to the position of several leading companies have given the country considerable trouble, but the anticipated collapse did not take place.

The Commonwealth of Australia presented for years a characteristic example of the evil effects of over-spending. Both Commonwealth Government and State Governments, as well as individuals, spent far beyond their means ever since the war, and the debts of the Dominion have become intolerably heavy. The system of basic wages adopted by the Socialist majority in the legislation raised the standard of living, and brought about a heavy increase of imports. When the crisis resulted in a fall in the price of the country's principal export products—wheat and wool—the penalties incurred by the unsound economic and financial policy soon became evident. The Australian pound depreciated greatly in spite of the effort of the authorities to support it by means of gold exports. Owing to the threat of the Socialist Government of New South Wales to repudiate its debts, the credit of the country declined, and it was increasingly difficult to meet maturities by means of fresh borrowing. It may be said that no part of the British Empire, and very few countries outside, were affected to such an extent by the crisis, during its early stages, as Australia. While in the case of most other countries neither the authorities nor the public can fully be blamed for the crisis, in the case of Australia both authorities and the public were largely responsible for it.

It is true that the one-sided nature of the Australian system of production has, in itself, made the Commonwealth position extremely difficult; but the fact that New Zealand, whose system of production is similar to that of Australia, was able to weather the storm much better, is evidence that the fault lies with the Australians themselves. As New Zealand and Australia are largely competitors as regards exports, and the former was handicapped by the depression of the Australian exchange, it may be said that the latter has stood the pressure as well as can be expected in the difficult circumstances.

Apparently the depreciation of the Australian pound has made both the authorities and the public realise the necessity of putting the country's finances on a sound basis. Genuine efforts have been made to balance the budget, by reducing expenses and reducing the interest on Government securities, and wages have been reduced to some extent. At the time when the rest of the world was approaching the climax Australia appeared to be on her way to recovery. The political changes in the Commonwealth, and especially in the State of New South Wales, have paved the way for putting finances on a sounder basis, and have already produced a gratifying effect upon the credit of Australia.

India was affected by the agricultural slump, the silver position, and political troubles at the same time. Possibly the latter are largely the outcome of the first two; for while it is difficult to stir up discontent in a prosperous country, the task of agitators is greatly facilitated by economic depression. To some extent local industries benefited by the boycott of British and other foreign manufactures, but this was far from sufficient to counteract the adverse effect of agricultural depression. As, however, the great majority of the population still lives in extremely primitive conditions, and produces the major part of its own requirements, the crisis affected them to only a slight extent. The same may be said to hold good as to the primitive population of Crown Colonies.

After the suspension of the gold standard the rupee remained linked with sterling, and the depreciation in relation to gold currencies has brought some relief to the economic situation. Local industries were able to compete more successfully with exports from Japan and other gold countries. The appreciation of silver has improved the situation of the population, much of whose wealth consists of hoards of silver coin and bars. In India the economic crisis has become aggravated by political troubles. At first the movement of civil disobedience caused unsettling effects, and more recently the fresh outbreak of Hindo-Moslem conflicts provided a source of uneasiness. As a result of the realisation of part of the hoarded gold, fresh purchasing power was created, which to some extent counteracted the evil effects of the political and economic crisis.

The Straits Settlements and other rubber-growing areas of the Empire were particularly affected by the slump in rubber. The attempt to maintain the price by means of restriction of output had been abandoned in 1926 owing to the unwillingness of Dutch rubber-growing interests to collaborate and the rapid increase in the output of native producers. The fall of prices occurred too late to prevent an undue expansion of production, as a result of which the price of rubber has fallen to a level at which it cannot be produced profitably. As Holland and the Dutch East Indies did not follow Great Britain in abandoning the gold standard, the rubber growers of British colonies were at an advantage as compared with their Dutch East Indian rivals.

Although South Africa was affected by the agricultural depression, she was compensated, to some extent, by the increased interest in gold production. As a result of the scarcity of gold and of the slightly better prices obtained by producers, the mining companies began to concentrate upon the increase of their output. As soon as the fall of prices brings about a reduction in the cost of production, it is expected that it will become profitable to exploit the poorer and abandoned reefs. This will be all the easier, as new processes have been invented whereby it is now possible to work profitably upon these poorer reefs. New reefs have also been discovered, and, although their significance has not yet been tested, it is certain that there is much less talk about the coming exhaustion of South Africa's gold supply than there has been for the past ten years. The prosperity of gold mines has more than compensated the Union for the depression in diamond and platinum production. It was expected that South Africa would follow Great Britain's example by suspending the gold standard, and mining interests and agricultural products have put considerable pressure upon the authorities to bring this about. For political reasons, however, the Union Government was determined to remain on a gold basis even at the price of heavy sacrifices. To offer exporters some compensation for the disadvantages of the appreciation of the South African pound in terms of sterling a system of subsidies to exporters out of the proceeds of new import duties has been adopted.

APPENDIX X

WHAT we said about India in Appendix IX. holds good also of most other Asiatic countries. In addition to the agricultural depression, they suffered through the depreciation of silver, and in some countries also through political troubles.

Japan was just beginning to recover from her severe crisis of 1927 when the slump occurred. In addition to general causes, troubles in China also affected her exports. Fortunately for the country, its industries were able to adapt themselves to changed conditions and, by means of producing textiles, etc., of inferior quality, they were able to capture several important markets from their rivals. Japanese textiles were at an advantage against the rival products of Europe in China, India, and in such distant markets as the countries of East and North Africa. The weak point of the Japanese economic situation was the silk industry; being engaged in the production of a luxury article, it was bound to be affected by the depression to an especially great extent. The banking position has made good progress towards consolidation. A great number of small banks have amalgamated or gone into liquidation. As a result, the economic depression did not bring about a banking crisis. After the suspension of the gold standard in Great Britain the yen was subject to strong pressure, as it was expected that Japan might follow the example. Moreover, the Manchurian conflict has also accentuated the outflow of funds. To relieve the pressure the authorities exported to the United States a considerable part of the gold reserve, and by such means the stability of the yen was maintained for two months. The economic situation of the country was unfavourably influenced by the Chinese boycott of Japanese goods, and by the uncertainties of the political situation. Finally, in December, the Government resigned, and the first act of the new Government was to prohibit the export of gold. The yen at once depreciated by about 30 per cent in terms of gold. In 1932 its depreciation continued, and by June it was quoted at a discount of about 25 per cent in relation to sterling. The weakness of the yen was due to internal and external political troubles, which resulted in an outflow of capital. It had a beneficial effect upon Japanese export trade, which was able to recapture its lost markets in the Far East and elsewhere.

In China, lack of political stability contributed to aggravate the economic difficulties. Although the Nationalist Government had succeeded in establishing itself all over China, its position was far from stable and its financial situation was highly unsatisfactory. Nationalism in the domain of banking and industry did not produce the results anticipated, and several local banks and industrial and commercial enterprises were unable to survive the crisis. The Government decided to abandon silver and to adopt a gold currency, but in the circumstances it was unable to carry out its scheme. The floods of the rivers in the summer of 1931 have inflicted misery and starvation upon a very large part of the population. Indeed, it has been one of the most deplorable aspects of the world economic crisis that while in America wheat was rotting in warehouses, in China millions of people were starving. The recovery in the price of silver has to some extent mitigated the crisis. On the other hand, the Manchurian dispute and the Shanghai conflict have added political difficulties to the economic troubles.

The Government's efforts to abolish the treaty rights of the western powers resulted in an efflux of capital, both Chinese and foreign; for the wealthy classes of the Chinese population, as well as of foreign merchants established in China, are not anxious to expose themselves to the corruption of the Chinese administration, and prefer to take refuge with their possessions abroad.

In Siam the economic crisis, together with unsound administration of the country's finances, has resulted in a budgetry deficit, and the Government was compelled to abandon the recently established gold standard. Attempts to raise loans abroad have failed, and it has proved impossible to lower the deficit with the aid of high taxation. In June 1932 a revolutionary movement compelled the King to agree to a constitution.

In Persia an attempt was made in 1930 to break away from silver and to stabilise the currency on a gold basis. As proper preparations for the change were not made, however, it failed, and the currency continued to follow the depreciation of silver. This, together with the political troubles and Soviet dumping, accentuated the difficulties of the country.

In Turkey the short-sighted anti-foreign policy adopted by the Nationalist Government drove out the productive and business elements of the population and deterred foreign capital and enterprise from taking advantage of the possibilities of the country. The repudiation of the debt agreement, concluded as recently as 1928, discredited the Government abroad. Unduly heavy military expenditure prevented it from carrying out its ambitious scheme of public works out of its own resources. Notwithstanding this, because Turkey is a primitive country, the economic situation did not become alarming, and Turkey succeeded in maintaining the stability of her currency without any external aid.

Egypt experienced a very prosperous period after the war as a result of the increased cotton production. Although she has not escaped the consequences of the depression, her cotton production did not suffer to the same extent as that of other countries, owing to the special quality of Egyptian cotton. The Egyptian Government followed the British example in suspending the gold standard in September 1931. The effect of the depression was comparatively moderate in the French and Italian possessions of North Africa.

APPENDIX XI

DURING and after the war Latin America experienced a period of prosperity and stability. Most of the Latin American states were able to meet their debt service and to stabilise their currency. It appeared as if Europe and Latin America had exchanged rôles; while the latter appeared to be becoming increasingly sound financially, the former was plunged into financial chaos. The efforts of the United States to secure a foothold in every Latin American country helped to increase their prosperity. American capital came flooding into Latin America in the form of industrial and commercial investments as well as Government and municipal loans. As a result, Latin American countries, especially the Argentine and Brazil, were able to import gold to a great extent during 1927 and 1928, and it appeared as if they would be able to consolidate their financial position. The Wall Street boom, however, checked American lending to Latin American states and also checked the wave of prosperity and progress. Ambitious schemes of public works and of the exploitation of natural resources had to be postponed and abandoned owing to lack of capital. The agricultural crisis dealt a heavy blow to the prosperity of the continent. The difficulties manifested themselves in the loss of gold acquired during the previous years, the depreciation of exchange, and the suspension of the gold standard by almost all Latin American countries, and their troubles culminated in a series of revolutions which broke out over the whole continent.

Brazil was affected by the crisis as seriously as any country in Latin America, and perhaps in the world; this was largely due to her one-sided system of production, for her prosperity depended too much upon coffee. The authorities attempted to maintain the prices of coffee at an unduly high level by means of restricting market supplies and accumulating stocks financed through external loans. Had all the coffee-producing countries co-operated with Brazil in a restriction scheme, and had fresh planting been prevented in Brazil itself, possibly the policy would have been successful; as it was, however, the efforts of Brazil to keep up prices led to an increase of production in other coffee-producing countries. Towards the end of 1929 the instability of the position became obvious, and the authorities had to allow the price of coffee to decline, and the exchange—which had been kept comparatively stable at the new parity for several years—also depreciated. In the autumn of 1930 revolution broke out and brought about a change of régime. The new Government decided to discontinue the policy aiming at bolstering up the price of coffee at an uneconomic level, and made desperate attempts to place the country's finances on a sound basis. Unfortunately the change of régime coincided with banking troubles in the United States, as a result of which American credits were suddenly withdrawn. Had it not been for the support given by British banking interests, the country would have undergone a complete collapse. As it is, it has become necessary to suspend the interest and sinking funds of most Brazilian loans, while the relative stability of the exchange has only been maintained by extremely stringent measures of restriction. In the circumstances, the execution of the reconstruction scheme elaborated by Sir Otto Niemeyer has been put aside to wait for better days. The Government has, nevertheless, made successful efforts to balance its budget. In January 1932 the Brazilian Government began the repayment of its short-term bank credit contracted early in 1931. There have also been several signs to indicate that conditions in the country have improved to some extent.

The Argentine by comparison suffered less than Brazil. Being an essentially agricultural country, she had to bear the full burden of the depression, but her system of production was better balanced than that of Brazil, and she also possessed a very large gold reserve to tide her over the difficult period. Unfortunately for her, during the first year of the crisis the Government was in the hands of an incompetent and corrupt dictator. Foreign capital was discouraged by the hostile policy of President Irigoyen. The floating debt increased to a very great extent and the exchange moved strongly against the country. Party politics dominated everything. For political reasons the Government attempted to break one of the leading banks of the country, a fact which duly characterises the lack of responsibility and unstatesmanlike attitude of the régime. The Government was overthrown by a revolution in the autumn of 1930, but the new régime was not sufficiently strong to carry out necessary reforms, and the task of financial reconstruction in the middle of an agricultural crisis was none too easy. In order to favour the interest of exporters, the Government allowed the peso to depreciate. When, however, the strain upon the exchange threatened to become excessive, restrictions were imposed upon foreign exchange operations. Thanks to its possession of a large gold reserve, the resisting capacity of the Argentine was, nevertheless, stronger than many other Latin American countries. In the summer of 1931, however, there was a sudden turn for the worse.

Conditions in Chile remained comparatively satisfactory in the early stages of the crisis. The Government was able to raise small loans abroad, and the rationalisation of the nitrate industry made good progress. The nitrate and copper situation, together with political troubles, have aggravated the financial situation of Chile, and the Government suspended the service of its debt. In June 1932 a revolution broke out and for a short time the Government was in the hands of Communists who aimed at confiscating foreign capital. Although this extremist Government was soon overthrown, the outlook remains none the less obscure.

Both Bolivia and Peru suffered a great deal from the fall in the prices of agricultural and mining products and through political troubles. Revolution followed revolution, and at the beginning of 1931 both countries were on the verge of bankruptcy. In Peru the leading local bank, the Banco del Peru y

Londres, suspended payment, and the new Government was unable or unwilling to support it in the interest of the external credit of the country.

In Colombia the stability of the political régime saved the country from similar troubles, while in Venezuela the wealth accumulated during the previous boom enabled the country to tide over the difficult period.

Central America was the scene of renewed political troubles. There was a revolution in almost every country. In Mexico, in addition to political troubles, the depreciation of silver aggravated the situation. The Government found itself incapable of carrying out the terms of the recently concluded debt agreement, and its creditors had to consent to a further scaling down of their claims and to the postponement of payment.

THE END

Printed in Great Britain by R. & R. CLARK, LIMITED, Edinburgh.

By the Same Author

BEHIND THE SCENES OF INTERNATIONAL FINANCE

Third Impression. 7s. 6d. net.

THE WEEK-END REVIEW.—"Its indictment is all the more damaging for being so largely a narrative of events. . . . A most valuable contribution to the literature of the crisis; in fact this is one of the few books on the depression which it would be a blunder to miss reading."

NEW STATESMAN.—"Dr. Einzig must know what he is talking about and should be in the position to obtain the facts. He has marshalled his case as a barrister would do, avoiding technicalities, reciting his points dispassionately and concisely, but concluding every argument with a most ferocious accusation. The effect is deadly."

FINANCE AND POLITICS

BEING A SEQUEL TO "BEHIND THE SCENES OF INTERNATIONAL FINANCE"

8vo. 7s. 6d. net.

MANCHESTER GUARDIAN COMMERCIAL.—"A valuable contribution to the inner history and inner meaning of international finance. . . . Dr. Einzig never minces his words, and there are times when one wonders whether he has overstepped the limits of reasonable criticism; but the facts which are marshalled in support are overwhelming."

WEEK-END REVIEW.—"With his earlier volumes it forms the most balanced, the most accurate, and the most justified by events of all contributions to the literature of the world crisis."

MACMILLAN AND CO., LTD., LONDON

BY DR. PAUL EINZIG

INTERNATIONAL GOLD MOVEMENTS. Second
Edition. 8vo. 7s. 6d. net.

MELBOURNE ECONOMIC RECORD.—". . . he has certainly
dealt faithfully with the subject . . . on which his book will doubtless
be regarded as the standard work."

THE NATION.—"Dr. Einzig combines in a rare degree three
separate gifts—he understands the technicalities of what goes on in
the City, he can explain it in a language intelligible to the ordinary
reader, and he can comment on it in terms which are interesting and
enlightening to the academic economist."

THE BANK FOR INTERNATIONAL SETTLE-
MENTS. Third Edition, revised and enlarged. 8vo.
10s. 6d. net.

THE STATIST.—"Among the books of particular interest to bankers
published this year pride of place must be given to Dr. Paul Einzig's
'The Bank for International Settlements'. . . . The book should be
of great service in extending knowledge of an important innovation in
the banking world."

THE FIGHT FOR FINANCIAL SUPREMACY.
Third Edition. 8vo. 7s. 6d. net.

INTERNATIONAL AFFAIRS.—"Dr. Einzig has given us a very
readable account of the influences at work in London, New York and
Paris to retain or obtain the leadership in world finance. . . . The book
can be confidently recommended to all who are anxious to follow the most
recent and interesting developments in international financial relations."

THE BANKERS' MAGAZINE.—". . . the author has given his
subject a dramatic interest rarely attached to treatises on finance."

THE WORLD ECONOMIC CRISIS, 1929–1932.
Third Edition. 8vo. 7s. 6d. net.

THE EVENING NEWS.—"A new Paul Einzig book has come to
be regarded in the City as something of a literary event. This rising
young economist has given us . . . the best explanation that has yet
been printed of the causes of the existing crisis."

THE SCOTSMAN.—"Mr. Einzig has recently written three short
monographs on current economic and financial problems of such outstanding merit that the reader will turn with interest to the present
volume on the economic 'blizzard'. Nor indeed will he be disappointed,
except in its excessive brevity."

MACMILLAN AND CO., LTD., LONDON